Girl Rearing

Girl Rearing

MARCIA ALDRICH

W. W. Norton & Company
New York   London

Copyright © 1998 by Marcia Aldrich

The text of this book is composed in Rotis Serif
with the display set in Weiss Italic.
Desktop composition by Stephen Ogata
Manufacturing by The Courier Companies, Inc.
Book design by Charlotte Staub

Library of Congress Cataloging-in-Publication Data

Aldrich, Marcia.
    Girl rearing / by Marcia Aldrich.
        p.   cm.
    ISBN 0-393-02748-1
    1. Daughters. I. Title.
HQ777.A67   1998
649'.133–dc21   98-5400
                    CIP

W. W. Norton & Company, Inc., 500 Fifth Avenue, New York, N.Y. 10110
http://www.wwnorton.com

W. W. Norton & Company Ltd., 10 Coptic Street, London WCIA 1PU

1 2 3 4 5 6 7 8 9 0

For Richard

Contents

For this, will mother go on cleaning house for eternity, and making it unlivable?

—ROBERT LOWELL

I

Alley

I was born in an alley. The one that ran behind our house on Twenty-second Street. The house sat balanced on the dead middle of the block, a brief plateau between dips at the cross streets and a long slope down to the main road. The house was a solid white colonial, renovated with a big picture window, lacquered black shutters, and a shiny brass door knocker. Our backyard, a big stretch of smooth green, also began quite level but slipped toward the edge of the lot and then, beyond the back fence, fell into a slide. From the rear of the house a path and set of steps led out from the porch and down to a detached garage. And behind the garage was the alley.

Obviously my birth didn't unfold according to plan. There was a plan, I'm told, a careful plan—it was a second marriage for both my parents—and they had seen to all the details. My father, an estate lawyer, boasted that a good will wasn't as airtight. The nursery, a converted den on the second floor at the back of the house, was ready. A bit dark, paneled in knotty pine, but more advantageously placed in relation to the master bedroom than was the pink room I later occupied, and the walls would muffle sound. The room was tastefully furnished and stocked with diapers and the standard powders and creams. Out in the hall, the obstetrician's number was posted unmistakably above the telephone. A small suitcase neatly packed with clothes waited in the closet near the front door. My father timed the drive to the hospital, that he might advise the doctor what minute they would arrive.

Then, two days before I was due, my mother's labor came on like a hard slap on bare skin. My father called the doctor and grabbed the suitcase and they hustled down the steps to the car. My mother worked herself into the rear seat to stretch out more comfortably. But no sooner had my father started to back out of the garage than she was overtaken with an irresistible urge to push. "Stop!" she panted. "I don't know if I can make it. Maybe we should go back inside." This triggered a debate between my mother and father, short but inconclusive, for while they teetered between coming and going, hospital and home, out I came, delivered unceremoniously to the world, without doctor or midwife, half on the backseat and half on the floor, squirming out the rear door and spilling into the alley. My mother screamed—whether to my father or me I'm not sure— "No, not here, for godsakes, not in the alley! Go back!"

An awkward beginning to my relations with the known world, that is, my parents. An awkward beginning to my story, too, for matters soon took an unpleasant turn. I didn't mind my birth—I was glad to be born, even if I was flung headfirst onto the floor— but it wasn't pretty. In fact, it was a mess, and no one hates a mess more than my mother. She cried and cried that I was all dirty, covered in filth, no better than a baby abandoned at the back of the Salvation Army.

She abhorred everything connected to my birth, with final contempt for the family automobile. We rode to the hospital in an ambulance, and when it was time two weeks later for my mother to come home, she insisted on a taxi, refusing to set foot in our car. "The very thought of it gives me contractions," she said. "I want it destroyed." My father didn't want to get rid of the car, not because he was attached to it, but because he liked to provoke my mother. For weeks it sat as it had been left, halfway into the alley. Eventually my father pushed it back into the garage, where neither he nor my mother ever ventured again. There it sat until the tires went flat, the seats molded, and birds built nests on the dashboard.

Alley

I stayed in the hospital longer than my mother. My meager weight and the unsanitary conditions of my birth kept me in isolation. With all the fuss to sanitize me, you'd think I had been born in a dumpster. My distaste for the orderly and clean began in those first days, when I lay on my back, helplessly strapped to an IV on the infectious corridor, in a glass cubicle under hot lights, getting angrier and angrier.

A baby cries in rhythm, especially the newborn, who spends all her breath on every cry, breathes, and cries again. No one answered, that is, no one came. My mother lay at home in darkness, cheated out of the birth she had expected. She didn't want any child of hers to be born where things grow without encouragement, license, or proper name, where untidy items are abandoned and messy dramas occur. She crossed out what reminded her of that day. She crossed out the car. Where photographs of the newborn were to be pasted in my baby book, she crossed out the blank spaces.

When it was time for me to come home, I was not entirely surprised by my installation in the wooden nursery. Who can say how soon a dark view begins? It was like the hospital, hot and solitary. There was even a corridor, a narrow passage that ran to the master bedroom. At the end of it, my cries were muffled, making rest possible for the other tenants. Or perhaps I believe that my father heard me in the middle of the night. It was he who sometimes came and lifted me onto his chest. I remember the feel of the moonlight, cool on my skin, through my parents' windows where he walked me.

My family has never gotten over the circumstances of my birth, and for a long time I believed that's why things turned out as they have. For my mother it was a sudden exposure of accident and disappointment; me it made resilient, solitary, receptive to chance and unmapped ways. An obligation fulfilled to a new husband, a repayment for his rescue, a gesture toward balancing the old with the new—my birth was a mistake, it accomplished none of these. My mother's X in the baby book marked a negative space in the portrait of my family.

But maybe an alley is just an off-route to the same place, a slow secret that leads where the main thoroughfare directs. Or maybe it goes someplace wholly new and unknown, or goes nowhere. What grows in the alley is unplanned, a darkness of blackberry thickets banked along the rim, coarse summer flowers that grow like weeds, smells potent as gasoline, stalks furrowed in dung, tufts of pickerel weed, the havoc of division, horsetails, and dust. And the alley is in me.

Balance

Their father, not mine, supervised the digging of an iron ore shaft in which, one afternoon, gas caught sparks and ignited. Their father, not mine, went down the shaft to save his men. Their father, when the shaft collapsed, not mine, suffocated, died, and was buried. That year a rash of grief ran down my mother's face, divided in two. My half sisters' father, not mine.

It was never talked about. Not his death, nor he himself. The wedding pictures, the portraits of babies, the snapshots of early married life were locked away in a suitcase pushed back to the farthest corner of basement storage. I was told, Never to go back there. I knew something terrible had preceded me.

They were young, Helen, Fran, and Gwen, toddlers and babies, when he died. What was their father like, what could they have thought of him? They had come along one after another, like letters of the alphabet, and they hardly knew him. He must have been a shadow, not much more real than he was for me. But he was theirs, and they were his and looked like him. My sisters were darker than I, with brown eyes and olive tones. In bone structure they recalled my mother; even as children they were long and thin and aristocratic, like my mother. But she was fairer in complexion, with hazel eyes.

When we visited his mother, their grandmother, I saw the one photograph of him in the gilded silver frame above the mahogany bookcase in the parlor. I instinctively knew it was their father, and that I shouldn't be caught staring. He was sitting on a large rock, a fishing rod loose in hand. He looked young, handsome, and alive—ready for some adventure. I watched to see if my sisters' eyes would travel to it. I thought my mother would be unable to avoid it, that she would run her fingers along its edges. But I never saw her stop before it; her eyes never turned in that direction. She would have preferred that his mother put the photograph away, as my mother herself had done. It was over, that chapter. Next to the photograph was another, my mother on her first wedding day. She wore a fine formal gown of creamy satin that pooled in graceful currents about her feet. A train cascaded from her head and swept behind her endlessly. She, too, was young, dreamy and radiant.

I never saw the house they lived in; they had lived in another town. When my mother remarried, they moved into the house on Twenty-second Street. When we visited my sisters' grandmother in the town they had lived in, I asked my mother if she would drive by their old house to show me. The answer was always the same: no. I tried to get her to describe the house, how big, what street. I could never draw her out.

I obeyed my mother's wishes; I never opened the suitcase. But I imagined an album of their life. There was a bungalow, nestled into a corner lot on a less-traveled road, perhaps unpaved. It was painted a pale yellow, like a faded daffodil, with white trim, white eaves, and a wisteria in lavender clusters festooned over the front porch. Every day one of my sisters checked the mailbox, perhaps the freestanding kind, out in front by the street. Helen or Fran skipped down the steps, opened the box, drew out the letters, and on her way back inside read where they were from. A little matching garage sat behind the house, at the end of the fenced backyard. The fence was white and had a latched gate. It wouldn't be high, but rather low and easy to climb over. The backyard would be small, with fruit trees, crabapple and pear, and lily of the valley in silvery clumps along the fence. My mother loved the scent of lily of the valley. A rope swing, good for a small child, hung from a strong limb. The seat would be smooth, blond wood.

Balance

There were young girls in the backyard, arranged about a small picnic table set with a child's tea service. Their dolls were company, everyone in her best party dress. My mother came out the back door and crossed the lawn from the house, carrying cups of tea in the wind. Her body was straight as a needle sewing through the waves of grass. Her long, graceful hands balanced the cups without a hint of danger. On the table, a tray of sandwiches, cut into little triangles, and small square lemon cakes. Blueberries swam in cups of cream, and the sugar bowl was passed without reserve. There was such delicacy in the lifted spoons. Yet no matter what fun they had, no matter how delicious the tea or beautiful the doll, they were listening . . . for their father's steps on the drive, to see him swing open the gate, a string of fish braided down his back. I watched them from my unborn position.

I stood beside the locked suitcase of my mother's early life. I imagined her younger. What she must have been in a room filled with red roses, and a carpet strewn with clothes from the night before! I saw her features and her husband's cut in the cascade of satin sheets, her hair fanning the pillow, her husband turned to see her breast. She borrowed the colors of the room, the roses, as she tossed on the bed. What they would say? Secrets for no one to hear but the spider, the thorn-spiked roses, the porcelain swans in their silent recesses. I smiled to think of my mother's flirtations, the silver combs on the dresser taken from her hair, the loose coins from his pockets. What would she say to him, what would she wish? There was no key I could use to unlock my mother's life. There had been love and happiness, I felt sure. Sometimes, perhaps, when no one was home, my mother went back to open the suitcase.

I don't know what my mother did to survive after his death. There wasn't much money. She was a widow raising three young girls, without assistance and without practical experience of life alone. Years passed before she would remarry and bear me.

Meanwhile, what of my father? Already divorced, he was selling life insurance to pay for law school. I have made up a scene of their meeting for the first time.

He called at the house to sell her a policy. After all, he must have thought, she should know the perils of loss. There is comfort in the belief that you have provided, he reasoned.

My mother was in the basement working with a noisy old wringer washer. She has told me about this washer, how hard it was to operate, how many diapers she washed. My father rang the doorbell, fidgeted with his papers a minute, knocked on the screen door and rang the bell again, and received no answer. He knew that she was home because he had telephoned to arrange the visit. Her car was in the driveway, and the front door was open behind the screen. He became concerned. In the time it took him to decide to enter the house, something broke in the washer and the basement began to flood.

When my father neared the kitchen, he heard my mother's "Oh no, oh no." He moved cautiously to the top of the stairs and called down, "Madam?" She was startled at first, then relieved, recognizing his voice. Coming down the stairs, he told her to hand up the laundry basket of clean clothes, and he carried them to safety. Then he stepped gingerly into the flood, which had materialized rapidly, picked her up in his arms, and lifted her into the kitchen. She was dripping and crying, both.

While my father didn't himself know how to fix the flooding, he knew the next best thing, someone who did. Having deposited my mother in a chair, he called a repairman. "You should always have the phone numbers of repairmen at hand, preferably taped on the wall," he said.

My mother nodded, warmed by his wisdom. "I am so grateful," she said.

Children wonder if they have been conceived in love, though they don't know exactly what that means. They think it is important to come into the world out of love and passion. But how can you be certain? Do three quick babies in a row show a want of planning? Or a sign of welcome to all? Well-spaced intervals of years look like intent, but when the gap before the last child grows too large, you suspect an autumnal surprise. Besides, what does a plan tell you about love?

We are born into circumstances whose history we cannot compute; nonetheless, we absorb them, embody them, in a skin we can never completely shed. No one ever said, *You are a disappointment. You cannot replace my father. You cannot make up for my dead husband. You are not our sister.* But it was so, a history steady and silent as my pulse, attending on my birth and shadowing me, one foot in life and one foot in death, precarious there, balancing.

No

My first word was "no." Before I said it, not even a grim baby talk of "mama" or "dada" could be construed. I was nearly three years old, and my family thought me defective or, worse, sullen, until the day my sisters, in exasperation and boredom, plunked me down on the piano bench and taught me to say no into an empty milk bottle.

Why a milk bottle? Helen and Fran had inspected me closely, palpating my lips under a flashlight, and concluded that they were flabby and indecisive. My sisters knew I needed rounded extension to bring off a no, and they showed me how. First Helen and then Fran puckered her lips into a perfectly open 0, raised the bottle ever so slowly for dramatic and pedagogical effect, and gripped the bottle's ridge with her lips. Arching her eyebrows to stress the simplicity of instruction, Helen said, "It's one, two, three, *no,* one, two, three, *no;* just blow *no,* just blow *no.*" With each no into the bottle the musical notes embroidered in red on the rim of her flared black flannel skirt tripped up the front, and her cinched waist grew even smaller. Then Fran took her turn and no'd so loudly that the top button of her sweater popped with the effort. Her no flew the length of the bottle and soared beyond.

Now it was my turn. I raised the bottle, pursed my lips, gathered my whole self into a *no,* and let it go. My no boomed into the bottle, and my sisters laughed and clapped their hands, cheering, "All right!" "*No,* sister!" and "Say that *no!*"

No sound I had ever produced rivaled the bomb of that first

no, and nothing had pleased my sisters as much. Once I got the hang of it, I could not quit. If they had wished, I was willing to say no into milk bottles endlessly. But they egged me on to bigger and better no's. Not yet three, I swaggered about the house, pronouncing no to the cat and no to the toaster and no to anything that crossed me. It became a game between my sisters and me, with greater variations as time went on. At the front door I was their sentry against unpopular neighborhood kids who asked, "Is your sister home?" On the phone I was their spokesperson against unwanted callers.

One day, perhaps the last I remember, we were in the side yard, hidden by box shrubs and crabapples, Fran and Gwen with their green and red hula hoops and I with mine—handed down to me by Helen, who had outgrown such silliness. They were teaching me hoops and cheers: "One, two, three, *jump*." With economical skill they put their hoops into motion, swiveling their hips with arms raised, O's circling in O's. They could make the hoops orbit as if of their own accord, effortlessly in unison.

"Girls!" We heard our mother calling from the house. Chores, piano, bedrooms. The hoops fell out of orbit and crashed to earth. "Girls!"

Fran and Gwen looked at each other. They put their hands on their hips, leaned toward one another, and with large ritual dips cheered, "No! no! no!" I joined in between them.

"Girls! Girls! Girls!"

"No! No! No!"

It volleyed between the house and the yard. We picked up our hula hoops and resumed, chanting "No, no, no" while rotating our hips. My hoop spun round and round, and I was deep in my reverie, and I could no longer hear my mother.

Our hoops almost touched, our worlds almost touched, our lives. For a few moments only, my girlhood reached to meet the tag end of theirs. But by then my sisters were teenagers. Helen was on her way to becoming a woman, rushing to become one it seemed to me, I was so far behind her. Fran and Gwen were poised to follow her trajectory.

The reverie ended when boys made an entrance. My sisters no longer implored me to say no. Instead they said no to me, followed up by "Scat, brat" and "Beat it, infidel." With boys my sisters began the yes phase. That to which they had formerly said no they now said yes. They were at odds with each other on all points except the importance of saying yes to boys. Their yes was ready-made, their lips like wire and pulleys. Any pimpled boy could set them going, lilting a metrical yes, yes, yes. If some sniveling boy asked them to swivel their hips, twist their bodies, and spin back, they would. Tom, Dick, or Harry appeared and strummed them, and they minded, oh how they minded— better than ever they minded our parents. They responded, trusting in something, being sure, secure in the deceptions of yes, the aggressive *y* and swishing *s* pushing the resistant *n* to a vanishing point back of their throats. Suddenly they were gone, gone to the world of boys and friends, to college, to marriage, to motherhood, to death.

Our lives barely touched before my sisters were gone. Their signs remained in the stained ovals on the wallpaper by the telephone in the upstairs hall, where they spent their best hours, whispering to the phone about boys. With hair wet, sometimes rolled up in a towel, they leaned back against the wall and cradled the phone in the curve of their long necks, until my father chastised them for tying up the line. And so they'd shake out their hair and brush it till the next call came, *Ring! ring! ring!* in the hall, always for them.

Yes

I slept in a room with windows that were never open.

I slept in a room with windows that did not open.

I slept in a room in which, as it was, the windows could not open.

From outside came the sounds of trains and automobiles in summer, birds in spring, children on sleds in winter, winds rustling in autumn. The sounds came through the windows and I heard them all. I did not miss the sounds, they were not unknown to me because the windows were not open. They were not kept from me. But I did not hear them cutting or deep, and hearing was knowing that the sounds came from beyond the closed windows, and beyond they were biting and high.

There were smells too, apples on the ground, ripe and withered, blossoms in the spring. But the smells did not come through windows that were never open.

The room was sometimes warmer in winter when the furnace blew air into it, sometimes cooler in summer when the air was cooled and conditioned, sometimes neither warm nor cool in the spring and fall.

In this room the windows had been painted shut. The frame and sash were coated with a lustrous pink. Not just a dash of pink here and there—a swirling pattern of pink roses on a white blanket I might have stomached. No. Every inch of wood was lacquered the pinkest pink. Pink hangers and pink liners for pink drawers, a pink shoecase hung from a pink closet door, pink light switches and pink doorknobs, a pink mirror and pink lightbulbs to bathe me in a pink glow. At night even the stars seemed pink.

I had no say in the matter. No one inquired, "Would you like your windows open?"

If someone had asked, I would have answered, "Yes, I want my windows open." To be sure, I would have preferred a room with more ventilation. I would have relished the affirmative. But it did not happen. No one asked my preferences. My sense of the windows did not factor.

I was installed in a room with a certain closed disposition, and that was that.

When my preferences did factor, there were limited options.

1. I could say yes and do what was set out for me to do.
2. I could say no and refuse to do what was set out for me.
3. I could go around, appear to say yes but really say no.
4. I could make myself scarce, being unavailable for parental scrutiny.

These were all of my options (or I could die). Each option had limited effectiveness, and I was forced to use them in combination. I did try to minimize saying yes. I did not want to say yes to the chances I was given. They were not what I wanted. But I could not say no, refusing what was set out for me at every moment. Clearly this was impossible. I had to agree, to say yes, but I agreed only to what I considered unimportant. Or such was my intent. I could not always or I rarely accomplished it because I could not predict what was important and what was not. Sometimes the important and the unimportant switched places.

I discovered that it is difficult to say no to requests formerly habitually agreed to, and if I had been saying yes to something when it was unimportant and it became important, I could not change. Sometimes, then, I started with saying yes because it did not matter and then it did matter, but I could not then refuse.

Fran and Gwen started saying yes and then they could not say no. They did what was set out for them. Helen appeared to say yes, but often she was saying no. She went around.

I never asked for a doll; dolls were given to me. Expensive, exquisite dolls. How then, being a girl, should I have refused? I pretended to accept them. I avoided the room where my dolls lived.

What was I supposed to do with them? A doll is a doll. It might get broken or worn out or lost; it might be thrown away or passed from hand to hand, but it would never grow up, or grow out of its clothes or shoes or house or name. It would never walk on its own two legs searching for food. It would never stand in the rain and remember. It would never open a window or climb a tree.

The dolls would always say yes.

They had perfected option number 1.

It was set out for me that there was pleasure in pulling a string to make the doll say, "Mama." There was pleasure in making a doll cry *real tears*. When my mother made me cry and I said, "Mama," I could comfort myself. I could perform the same upon my dolls.

I did not want to play with my dolls. I never wanted to do to others what had been done to me. I never wanted to repeat, repeat, repeat. I wanted to say no.

The dolls were model daughters. A doll always says yes to what is set out for it to do.

It was set out for me: "Be grateful. Show pleasure"—at the dolls' blank faces mounting the shelves of my dresser. The dolls, a whole silent galaxy of them, sat enthroned on the dresser in my pink room. We were often confined together. They surveyed my childhood; we met each other's eyes. They were dead, not alive. Nothing would ever transform them.

When I brushed up against them, their miniature eyes blinked. It was set out for me to be caught up and carried away in the ribbons and tea set no hunger could break. To set a tea before the doll to say yes to.

I arranged them on the floor with the door open so that my

mother could see. I changed their outfits and shoes, lifted a tiny cup to their closed pompadour red lips. Show pleasure at the touch of a doll's polished skin was the order of the day. Don't refuse the doll with the long blond flip.

To refuse the doll of the long blond flip was to slap my mother. To push the doll with perfect incisors into the oven and set the timer was to slap my mother. To dig a hole in the backyard and bury the doll of platinum flips in sullen soil was to slap my mother.

Instead I gathered the doll with no baby fat to lose, her porcelain pallor smooth. I praised her obedience—"Aren't you a good girl"—and watched her mount the shelves of my pleasure. The dolls never engaged with feeling.

I practiced saying no to myself, with the dolls watching, rehearsing. I told myself—just open your mouth and say no. If I didn't say no, I didn't know exactly what would happen. I felt I would dissolve, lose my shape, my volume, my ability to speak. I could not say yes, it felt like betrayal. I said yes to make people happy. I went around. I said yes because I thought it was not important this time. Yes: I will do what you say.

I dreamed my bed rose up and glided out the window. I flew all over the world while my dolls sat monotonously on the dresser.

Eventually my mother gave the dolls to my nieces. They were passed on in superb condition, with extensive wardrobes.

Call

In the evening my mother stood on the back porch, facing the fence and the alley behind, and rang the bell, calling me home. She rang a long time in steady, even peals; she never varied or intensified her ringing, even when she saw no signs of me and did not know whether I had heard. She didn't know; nevertheless she did not change the way she rang the bell.

Sometimes she called my name. Her voice, high and musical, floated above the grass, sloped down to the fence. It came to me like a gift. But I never came right away, never made my presence known, never answered her call. Why did I let her stand, waiting for what would not come? Why didn't I call out, "Here I am?" Wherever I was, I stopped, I stopped moving. Sometimes I moved my lips, but no sound emerged. I could see my mother, but she could not see me. I was covered by the darkness of blackberry along the rim of the alley. She looked stately, neat and clean, and slightly foolish. Her house was polished, groomed with its black shutters freshly painted, the white sides washed.

My mother would not look for me. She would not step off the porch into the grass and cut across the long expanse of yard; she would not climb down the hill to the alley. The grass might be wet; she might be inappropriately dressed. She would not walk the fence line searching. She would not lean upon the fence and squint into the alley. She would not set foot there, this I knew. Instead, she went back inside.

As daylight died away, I watched the lights of the house go on. No one moved from room to room, no one looked out a window. My mother would not run out in her nightgown, the skirt wrapping awkwardly about her legs; she would not entreat me. She would not say, "Come home, out of the alley, the water is running, it's time for your bath." Or "Come home, I have chocolate treats." She would carry nothing in her hands. She would not make a spectacle of herself. She would not cajole, bribe, or promise me things she knew would never come. She would not give me a false impression of the life yet to be. I rang the bell, she said, now let her come or not come.

My mother took the bath, sat down to supper in silence with my father and sisters, and then turned down the bedclothes. She thought: what have I given birth to? She is not a fox or a runaway dog, no wild animal or stray prowling the alley. I will not lick her clean.

I did not come when my mother called. I looked at the closed windows, my mother's arm lifted striking the bell, I heard her voice call my name, and I stepped back into the alley, farther and farther, until I disappeared.

Dirt

Girls are not born with a devotion to sanitation. When I was a young girl, dirt intrigued me: dirt under rocks, dirt under fingernails, dirt in vacant lots. Cobwebs, fallen moths, and anthills were my world. I liked to run my hands and press my lips against a freshly cleaned windowpane to leave my mark. I liked the presence of dirt, its inevitability on my fingers. After a summer's day of exploration, keeping the dirt of the day close to me was keeping the day itself alive. For dirt is something, and cleanliness is nothing.

But at the end of the day I was not allowed to remain as I was. Dirt was what my mother tried to keep out of the house, and I was its prime carrier. When I was forced to come inside, I spent a lot of time washing my hands.

My preschool teacher approached that sort of dirt systematically. She said it was never too early to develop good lifelong habits. She insisted that we wash our hands according to the medical model.

Say it and do it was her method of training. She stood before a child-sized sink at one wall of the classroom, with a wide, shallow steel pan, a towel, and a bar of soap on the counter next to the sink. A clothes tree nearby held layers of tiny vinyl aprons, plus one adult size.

She talked us through the model, performing each step for us, using slow, exaggerated motions. There were thirty-nine steps, counting the fingers.

"Questions?" she asked.

My arm went up. "Why do we have to wash our hands?"

"To be clean and to keep clean. Cleanliness," she said, as if reading from an enormous dictionary, "is the state or condition of being or keeping clean."

I looked at her, puzzled. Being—or keeping? If you were clean, why did you have to keep clean?

In her own person and domain my mother came as near to being clean and keeping clean as humanly possible. The foundation of cleanliness, the first law, was to make no mess. I didn't live in the house—I visited it like a museum, with my mother as docent. On one guided tour of my life, she pointed out that I must be clean *and* orderly. "You must address both when you strive for cleanliness," she warned. "One's windows may shine, but one won't have a truly clean house when a mess lies about." This apropos of my bedroom.

Yet when my mother cleaned, she was gloomy, angry, as if she regretted the cleanliness of our house. She'd see dirt where I saw none. "Look at this filth!" she'd spit out with disgust, pointing through the doorway to some gleaming floor. She was especially irritated when she woke from her dreams with a list of tasks in her head: hang up clothes, vacuum, empty the lint screen in the dryer . . . Sometimes the list was *clean house*. These were times of trouble, mornings when she was most out of control. If she didn't dust by noon, there wouldn't be an afternoon. She would panic and begin cleaning several areas at once. As she dusted the mantle, she noticed smudges on the windows in the dining room and from there glimpsed dust gathering in the corners of the vestibule. Rushing to the kitchen for a dust mop, she spotted handprints on the wall and gathered a sponge and used it to wipe coffee stains from the cabinets. She cleaned as if the house were a mosaic, fragments of dirty surfaces, like the pieces of colored tissue paper we glued to posterboard in art. What was the danger she was in? My heart beat fast for my mother; she must be relieved of dirt.

I decided to ask Mrs. Galloway, a novelist, who lived down the street—hers was a carnival funhouse. You couldn't predict what you might sit on or discover running across the walls. Nine intact piñatas hung in an upstairs bedroom. Closets were not safe to enter, for something would fall on your head—something very possibly worth discovering, a valuable old lampshade or a beautiful African mask. Her pleasures were those of accumulation. Cleaning would require she throw things away. "How would I decide what stays and what goes?" she asked.

My mother used to say, "I doubt Mrs. Galloway knows where anything is. How could she?" But looking back on it, I see that Mrs. Galloway was a genius of collection, who stashed. Records had no arrangement, not by composer, artist, instrument, or period. Yet when asked for a certain book, a back issue of a magazine, an old Halloween costume, or props for a play, she disappeared into the heart of the house and reappeared with the object. Her typewriter was set up in the living room. Pages of her stories were strewn across tables and baskets of sleeping cats, the stationary bike and the collection of ceramic eggs, across the pile of utopian literature she'd been building up since she was a girl. When she wanted to pull a story together, she circulated the house, culling pages from lampshades, potted shrubs, the bones of skeletons left from Halloween. She always managed a complete copy.

Mrs. Galloway's house wasn't just disorderly, it was also plain dirty. Dead flies from summers past lay in crinkled piles on windowsills. When we visited, my mother held herself apart, trying to stay clean. One day we were there for lunch, and my mother was standing stiffly in the kitchen, giving her usual nervous glances at the reigning mess.

"Go wash your hands before lunch," she told me.

I saw my chance. I asked Mrs. Galloway, "Why do we have to wash our hands?"

My mother broke in. "That's a silly question. To reduce the danger of infection, of course."

"Not so silly," Mrs. Galloway replied. "You think clean is good, dirt is bad. Cleanliness is good because it's clean. Dirt is dirty."

"That's self-evident."

"It's not self-evident to me," said Mrs. Galloway. "It's like gardening. Things need a soil in which to grow. Put down your rags and broom! Throw open the doors and windows and welcome what would come in!"

As she was clearing a place on the table for a plate of sandwiches, she knocked over a pot in which a geranium had passed away. "Cleaning produces cleanliness," she said, paying no attention, "the most transitory of productions. Keeping clean is impossible. Dirt does not cease to exist. It just goes somewhere else. Can't you see that?"

"I can see that," my mother said, eyeing the table and edging away. She backed up toward the wall and, forgetting herself for a moment, touched it and got grease on her sweater.

"Houses and families are things into which dirt flows, and you cannot push it out except at some cost," Mrs. Galloway said. "Many unhappy families live in clean houses. Look at the Smiths." With the edge of her hand she brushed the spilled soil onto the floor. "Sit down here, M."

We lived next door to the Smiths, a woman with a grim mouth, a grunting husband, two school-age children—a rather oval daughter and a wan, angular son—and a nasty silky terrier. I cannot speak to the condition of the inside of the house—I never saw it—but the exterior was immaculate. It might have been autoclaved. Mrs. Smith washed the windows inside and out twice a week. She cleaned the driveway daily, regardless of the weather. In autumn, with the red leaves drifting in clouds, no fallen leaf rested upon her driveway. Still in her housecoat and slippers, she emerged with the silky and vanquished the leaves one by one, picking them up and pinning them in her hands. She was manifest destiny, sweeping the tribes westward, the silky yapping at their heels. Each morning year round she carried out the same small coil rug and rectangular mat, hung them on the clothesline, and beat them viciously with a broom for long angry minutes. When the rug and mat were sufficiently pulverized, she hauled them back inside. On school days, the son and daughter then exited the back door and slumped disconsolately up the alley. Mrs. Smith and the silky drove off for an ice cream.

"The average American woman spends twenty-eight hours a week chasing dirt," Mrs. Galloway was saying. She hesitated a moment. "Of course I'm not sure just which activities around the house this figure includes, because cleaning—well, it's like other things people want, it has indefinite edges."

"What on earth do you mean?" my mother asked, wiping at her sleeve with a wet sponge. The sweater looked done for.

"Does dumping the cat box count as cleaning or pet care? What about a trip to the store to buy soap and sponges? Hauling the bottles out of the basement is getting your deposit back, I suppose, not cleaning." Mrs. Galloway was thinking out loud now. "Laundry maybe yes, ironing probably no. But for the sake of argument, let's lump it all together: dusting, vacuuming, sweeping, gathering trash, taking the cans out to the curb, bringing the cans back to the garage, returning empty bottles to the store, stacking newspapers, washing floors, windows, sinks, bathtubs, toilets, counters, changing sheets and towels, washing hanging light fixtures and TV screens, picking wax off candlesticks. At twenty-eight hours a week, fifty-two weeks a year, that's . . ." She pulled open a drawer, took out paper and pencil, and made some calculations. "That's 1,456 hours a year. Let's say the average woman begins to clean at age twenty-one and cleans for the next fifty-five years . . ."

My mother said, "Finish your sandwich, M. We have to go."

"The average American woman spends twenty-eight hours a week chasing dirt," Mrs. Galloway resumed, "and she does not ask what she does or why she does it. She cleans without question."

"Oh really, Louise," my mother said, "your imagination has run away with you this time, quite away. Stop waving that paper in my face. I clean because it is the right thing to do. Write this down in your book—*the wisdom of one's own home.*"

As my mother and I went up the street, I thought about two

chrysanthemums my mother had planted last year. One came back in the spring and the other did not. Some seeds took hold, some didn't. I didn't know why.

Helen

Helen was an unanswered question. She was the tracing of a sister, not the thing itself, and I tried to fill in her outline.

She resembled Fran and Gwen, but there was a difference. They were well behaved; she seemed well behaved. Like them, she carried herself well; that is, she was stately and held her head up high. But there was a difference. Perhaps the burden of being the firstborn set her apart, though you would not think a year would make a difference. But it was there. On school mornings, Fran and Gwen busied themselves in a flurry, readying their rooms for my mother's inspection, believing, it seemed to me, in what they were doing. Down the hall, Helen's room was neat but empty. I never witnessed her straightening up or making her bed, yet it had hospital corners, just as my mother had instructed. By the time I woke up and looked in, the room was

Yes.

Yes, she carried herself with pride, too much pride.

already ordered to perfection, and Helen had left for school.

 Her room, next to mine, was painted robin's egg blue, moody and changeable as the light and weather. Some days it seemed inviting, a tranquil lake warmed by the sun. Then, when Helen left, it turned celestial and cold, the color of frozen milk. Opposite the door stood a vanity with a tall mirror, where she did her hair. Under its glass top she slid dried corsages and sometimes the program, too, from proms she had attended. White organdy formed the vanity's skirt, and the same white organdy made the curtains, stiff and fussy, that hung at the windows, one of which looked out on the small side yard, where a crabapple tree with flowers a crushed red, profuse in spring, torqued up. She could step out the window into the tree's thronged branches. It was strong enough for climbing: its sturdy limbs easily held a girl like Helen.

 When she was gone, I did not enter her room, but looked in from the doorway. From there, leaning against the frame, I saw myself broken in the tall mirror, my torso floating unattached above the dried flowers of her vanity.

 When Helen was in her room, she allowed me to come in. I liked to feel and consider the mysteries and lights

Perfection.

Yes.

What did Helen see when she sat before it?

Not fussy, feminine.

It was a beautiful tree in the spring.

of her closet. On the inside of the door her shoes hung in their matched pairs. Her clothes were arranged by type, skirts in one group, blouses in the middle, prom dresses in plastic bags at the far end. She had a number of prom dresses, in many shades. They were strapless—I knew that was the fashion—with stiff flounced skirts to emphasize cinched waistlines. I didn't care for the prom dresses; Helen looked so old as she waited for her date to pick her up. I was interested in a particular white blouse, there, in the middle, a cross between a man's tailored button-down and a woman's fluid blouse; of an airier finish than the starched cotton of an oxford, and of a material, I thought, that would not cling or collect electricity. It did not shine like silk. I had never seen her wear it, but that is how I liked to think of her, in this white blouse.

She looked lovely.

I remember the blouse, a gift that she never wore.

Neither of us was at home much. I hung about the alley or wandered the open fields that backed onto our street of houses and ran wild down to the river. Helen was the lead cheerleader at school, on the swim team, a camp counselor, one of the most popular girls. Though she was wanted at home, though my mother called for her, regretting her absence—"Where is she *now*?" my mother would cry—she had places she'd rather be. I

Never so much as now. Yes, but she too was uncomfortable in the house.

37

believed that her tremendous success at being a girl made others desire her and draw her away.

At home, she was on the phone, laughing her reckless laugh or speaking in hushed tones that stopped abruptly when someone walked through the hall. Or she was arguing with my father over some upcoming social event (in spring of her junior year she was given a curfew and soon violated it). Or boys stopped by to search her out. That was when I liked to make a pest of myself. It was one way I could capture her attention, for sometimes we passed on the stairs as if I were an invisible unknown. I followed them wherever they went, a few paces behind. I liked to sit in a chair in the living room where they sat talking, never involving myself in their conversation, observing. Though Helen called it spying, I kept her secrets. I was her self-appointed chaperon, a role I took seriously—I did not know these boys and did not trust them—until Helen's furious protestations summoned my mother. She would send me to my room or outdoors with the admonition to occupy myself till dinner.

I often visited the white blouse. Long-sleeved, it let in light and breeze, with cuffs that buttoned, but not heavily. It had a simple, straight

Always on the phone. That laugh would get her in trouble.

You don't know the half of it.

It was presumptuous, making yourself a pest. Why did you concern yourself?

It was just a blouse, only a blouse.

collar that neither buttoned nor held its own distinct shape. The body was cut fuller than a man's dress shirt, with short, easy-to-tuck-in tails. No frills, no sheerness. It wasn't a blouse like lace curtains. It was dove white, the white of puffballs in May, without a hint of yellow.

One night of that curfewed spring, when everyone had gone to bed, I lay awake, uncomfortable in my pink room, and heard the faint noise of conspiratorial voices. I sat up, went to my window, and watched as Helen came out her window and climbed down the tree, one branch to another, shaking its red petals. I could make out only a wavy shape at the bottom. Down she went to meet a boy, down and down, setting the tree on fire. She leaped from the last limb to the ground, and in the dark she was jumping into cool moonlit water. I went back to bed, my eyelids heavy with secrets. In the morning her bed was perfect and the room cold.

Helen had a string of boyfriends, and I took their calls for her countless times. But I remember only the boy at the bottom of the tree. I did not know then who he was, just the boy who drew my sister out the window. And that he gave Helen a kitten. She named her May and then neglected her. Sometimes she fed her,

It was a lovely room. I painted it myself.

Don't speak of him.

I never knew where she came from. May, for spring and hope.

sometimes not. I liked to carry May to the fir tree beside the garage in the afternoon and stroke her head.

My parents' room was down the long hallway. They didn't hear her open the window and descend. If they had known of her nocturnal descents, they would have put a stop to her opening the window and climbing down. She would have been given a lifelong curfew.

Would we lie in our beds, knowing, and let her go? Why didn't you tell us?

In October, when May was teetering between kitten and cat, she disappeared. One day she was not there in the house or yard to greet me when I came home from school. I searched, and when Helen came home, we searched. I told Helen she probably had gone to the fields, attractive to strays of all sorts. The weather was turning, and we put on coats and crossed the fields. The wind was on my cheeks, and my hair whipped across my eyes. Helen wasn't much good at searching, but I knew to lead her down to the river. She tramped heavily through the brush at its edges, stopping more than moving forward, and calling, *Where are you, May?* At last I heard a weak cry and found her caught in a trap set for some larger animal. Helen undid the clasp and carried her kitten home.

I looked, too.

May's leg had been badly hurt, but the injury seemed local, and we thought she would recover. At first she looked to be mending. She was able to limp outside to sleep under the afternoon sun that warmed her curled body. But two days later when I sat down to rub her head, she did not move. I brought her inside and set her on the kitchen table, and my mother said she was dead. I carried her back outside and sat with her under the fir tree until Helen came home. She said the injuries must have been deeper than we could see. Together we buried May in the back-yard.

That winter I wore the white blouse. I knew Helen never would. Outside was a river with ice on it; the snow was enameled under the moon hung in a blue afternoon. I went into the room and opened the closet. There it was, the white blouse, hang-ing still, untouched, unmoved, in its reckless, secretive folds. Helen had suited the blouse so well. Could I? What would happen to it? Would it keep for the day when someone had grown into it? Would it be given to Fran and Gwen? Would I want to keep it? Would its presence shadow mine, in a drawer, in a closet, on my back?

I stood before a mirror in a blouse that was not mine and that hung on my frame. I could not touch the thought around me, and my heart was on fire. It was Helen's, it

The last winter before she graduated from high school.

I never disturbed her closet.

Should it be put in a drawer or torn to shreds?

belonged to Helen. The fit of the blouse would not be righted by a smaller size. It was made for the shape of a young woman, whose shoulders were broad enough to fill these empty spaces, whose arms were long enough for the cuffs to end at the wrists, not cover her hands, whose waist tapered. I disappeared inside the white blouse.

Could anyone bear to watch someone else in Helen's blouse?

X

I don't like the letter my name begins with—it falls unnoticed in the middle of the alphabet; the thirteenth and most unlucky letter, smack-dab in the mediocre middle, equidistant from A and Z. It looks like a caterpillar inching along. It conjures up images of mushy melodrama and malapropism, tendencies I sometimes evidence. It reminds me of Marilyn Monroe, stuck in her cabin's porthole and smiling mindlessly to the passengers who meander by, a voluptuous but farcical fate not entirely unimaginable as my own.

When my name is called, I don't think anyone is talking to me. When I hear my name, I have to shake myself to answer. On the phone, I want to say, "Wait, I'll get her."

My name was the one John couldn't stop calling until everyone in America dropped dead of boredom. It was an ostrich with its head buried in the sand. A name that spoke to a girl of mushrooms, misery, and mistakes, to a woman of meters running. My name was the girl before she takes off her glasses and unpins her hair and throws away that horrible cardigan sweater. My name was the woman who phones to confirm your appointment for a root canal, or the agent who tries to sell you a house beside the freeway.

I asked, "For what does this name prepare me?"

My family shortened my name, but not to a term of endearment. It resisted all alterations, like aluminum siding. It was always said one way, like *God*.

I asked my parents if I had been named after anyone, someone in the family, a close friend, a historical figure. Anyone? I wasn't particular. I wanted my grandmother's name, though my mother's memories of her mother were unhappy; despite her tragic end, I wanted the name of my mother's beloved childhood friend who died in an automobile accident. I wanted to be named after someone, after Isadora Duncan. A name like a long red scarf, a slash across time.

But I wasn't given that name. My beginning connected to nothing, to a crossed-out space in a baby book.

As it turned out, my parents hadn't considered a name for a girl because they hadn't planned on one. They had three girls already, and that was enough. When I appeared, each sluggishly came up with one name; they didn't agree, and they picked something in the middle.

Within the limits of my mother's recollection, she knew no one with my name. It belonged to no person of note, it had no associations. There was no particular sense of destiny evoked by its sound. No maternal hopes were embodied.

"I can't remember now why I liked it," she said. "I think because I didn't know anyone by that name. It was the novelty, I suppose."

My father preferred a very different name, short and plain, beginning with one of my favorite letters, *A*, an exact letter, all the vectors connected, which points upward with purpose. Named that name, I too would head in an upward direction.

But perhaps I admired the name only because it wasn't mine.

I knew three sisters, each with a very ordinary name, who did not brood over it. Their mother's name was Uranium, though everyone called her Jiggy. She and her poodle Cheri orbited a different sphere, one of flaming crêpes suzette, cocktails before dinner in the garden, red racing cars, and high, ringing laughter. How could a Uranium name her daughters so commonly? How could her daughters not envy her? As it happened the father, who was John, bestowed the names without his wife's assistance. He did not understand that the names he chose were dull. Yet not one girl voiced disappointment in a life lived with a name featureless as a geometrical solid.

Ordinary, conventional, uninspiring—so I would have judged the prospects had I borne one of their names. "What can come from it?" I would have asked.

I made up lists of replacements for my name. There were names that tried to strike a balance between girl and boy—names like Heller, Haley, and Honor. These began with a hard letter, bespeaking firmness and strength. *H* resembled *A*. I thought about heroine, house, home, hell, hill, hightops, hiccups, hornets, hostage, hilarious. Helen. The letter had possibilities.

The three ordinary sisters dismissed my strategies as a moody instability, a morbid self-preoccupation that would turn out badly.

"We don't see anything wrong with your name," they said.

To which I responded, "It doesn't suit me."

They could not fathom a name that didn't suit. A suitable name was one that wore well, like a good handbag. Their names would show few signs of use. But I was not interested in durability; I was after something less tangible. I needed a new name, a name that wouldn't bore or sound overly personalized—nothing too cozy or familiar. I wanted a name for which I could imagine interesting accessories. I wanted a name that named me and yet suggested the impossibility of entirely naming me. A name with a long history of multiple possibilities; a name galvanized, a name one approached with a mixture of caution and curiosity, a name that burst along the veins, pitched forward, pitched ahead. Not a name like violets strategically limp on a prom queen's wrist, not a name iced through the night, too perishable, too dear. What was wanted, what was wanting was a name that survived—a name like buds that suffer heat with but one lip curling, a signature of sorts, two crossed stems. A name that traversed itself and went in contrary directions, yet for all that, greeted itself at the journey's end—an old, bent woman and a young girl who had had to stand up straight, walking the same path.

When opportunities to rename myself came along, I seized them. When I went to summer camp at seven, I introduced myself as Aurora. None of the campers knew the difference, and the counselors, even my sister, were too busy to bother. When we made the traditional wish on the last night of camp, I wished under my chosen name, and it was Aurora's future that beckoned me. When the next day my mother came to pick me up and take me home, I didn't want to go. It was something of an embarrassment. She stood by the station wagon, still waiting for me to appear after all the other campers had been collected and driven away. I was running through the woods, the counselors chasing me and calling *Aurora! Aurora!* as if in ecstatic pursuit of the dawn.

Swimmers

For some, swimming begins as an instinct, a response of movements and emotions that the sight or feel of water evokes. Just look at some children: before they walk, they swim in rhythms on the floor and through the air, and their first word is *water*—water is their home. I was not the kind of strong swimmer who sens0ed the luster of the lake from the beginning. I had to learn what my sister always knew.

Helen at five was no longer content with the wading pool my mother had set up in the backyard. She wanted something deeper, a bottom she could not reach, to dive and see from that point of view.

"She didn't have a scrap of fear running through her," my mother told me. "I had to be on guard since she was a baby charging for the ocean."

Not just fear, I think—a wish for that other world where we can only live dangerously, or briefly, or not at all.

"Once she was busy finding stones and waded farther out than she should have," my mother said. "A wave knocked her over, and she could not get back on her feet."

Suspended under water, her suit billowing. Her dark hair limp and streaming from her face, as skin pulls away from the bone after weeks of immersion. Helen had already begun to decay, to begin the transfer.

"It took forever for me to reach her and pull her up hard out of the water. I wasn't gentle; I was rough." Jerking her back. "She coughed mouthfuls of water and then cried like the little scared girl she was."

But something had touched her. The veins in her eyelids bloomed like irises, the most delicate of shades. Something had begun to burrow inside her and beat as it must have beat inside my grandmother. My mother did not see that she would have to let her swim.

The summer after I turned seven I attended camp for the first time, and Helen was in charge of the waterfront. She had worked summers there all through high school and had a reputation for long-distance swimming. Of all the counselors, she alone wore a purple cap, because only she could swim the length of Lake Miranda.

Those chill hours, we'd be in and out of the water all morning. Wrapped in my brave new name, Aurora, I shivered on the diving float, where my unit assembled in the early light of the first dawn, flapping my arms in rough imitation of the strokes my sister sketched forcefully on the sheet of water below. I watched her dive from the dock into slate-cold water. She could hold her breath longer than anyone, and she disappeared for what must have been a full minute before she bobbed up a great distance away, farther than I could throw a ball in two or three tries added together. She swam back and staggered a little in the shallows, disoriented, before she gained steady land.

When she was in the water, it looked blue and inviting. The water held the wake of her breaststroke, churning heated figure eights. The cunning of her movement, her easy breathing, her rhythmic drive through deep water like a marine creature—this was a glimpse of beauty. But then, each morning of the summer, we switched places. She stood on the float above us, shouting instructions, while my unit flailed in the lake, again cold and gray without her. Again and again, day after day, she called me to the float, singled out my failures and my successes, and forced me—a baleful wedge of chattering cold flesh—to try it again.

Late in the summer I stopped thrashing and started to swim.

My mother was not much of a swimmer. I don't mean that she did not enjoy swimming—she did, as one enjoys the occasional game of croquet. But she was not much good at it. She was not athletic or strong, and she could not swim very far. She was not a force in the water.

She did have an identifiable approach to swimming, principles of routine procedure. The pace and manner were hers alone. She went slowly, with caution and restraint, with what she would have called dignity. She rose from her lawn chair or towel, picking up her bathing cap casually, and walked on long, thin legs gracefully in the direction of the pool (she would not swim in rivers, lakes, or oceans). She pointed her toes, almost kicking out as she walked, except that no one could call it kicking because the motion of her leg was so evenly executed. On a beach she would have raised no sand. As she stepped and pointed her toes in her slow, zigzag motion, she tucked her hair into the cap, fingers extended and deft.

When she arrived poolside, she lowered herself gently and tested the water with a toe—water too cold was a shock to be precluded. Gradually she acclimated her foot to the temperature, then moved body part by body part up from the feet until she had eased in up to the chest. There she stopped. Gauging depths, she held her arms out of the water and hopped, again with caution, away from the side. After a respectable period of adjustment, she began her measured stroke, holding her head just above the water and cracked to the side. As she sidestroked slowly across the pool, her head remained immobile, eyes fixed as if on some distant sun. Having reached the edge, she rested for a moment before turning around and swimming on her other side in the opposite direction. Thus she went, from one side to the other and back, always across the short dimension of the pool. She never swam the length; to lengths she had an aversion.

Some swimmers are like dancers, concentrating their energies and prowess into the economical propulsion of their bodies through the density of water. My mother's swimming was like pulling away the excess dough around a cookie cutter, the outline rather than the center of power. She was swimming, but she wasn't swimming. She seemed uncannily effective, a genius perhaps, at avoiding the fact of herself in water. She never submerged her head. I don't know what I would have done had I seen my mother plunge into a pool. I suppose I would have thought the worst—that she was trying to harm herself or had lost her mind, I'd grown so used to equating my mother with a life of checked emotion, risks untaken, avoidance of exhilaration.

When she removed herself from the water, she was never exhausted. She was never spent in the singular way swimmers spend themselves. She walked away from the water just as she had walked to it, removing her cap rather than putting it on. She did not collapse onto her towel or heave into a chair. The water having drained away during the slow stroll of return, it was unnecessary to dry herself, and she eased into her former position.

As for my own swimming—well, it hardly bears much discussion. It was middle-of-the-road, or middle-of-the-lake, swimming. I liked to hold my breath and duck my face into the water, for a few seconds at first, then a little longer. After a handful of sessions I could get my whole body under and kick myself forward a bit. But the lake was ready always to refuse me, to push me out and up to the air. I didn't really mind, for the light failed a yard under the surface, and I feared what was down below. A swimmer could get caught in the long roots, maybe, that wandered into the water from the trees at shore, though I never got deep enough to see any roots. How terrible to catch one's feet there, to feel one's lungs burst just below the bright world. So I dove a little and rose gratefully each time to the surface to swim again under Helen's eye, like a sun.

My grandmother, my mother's mother, was an excellent swimmer. She died of a heart attack before I was born, and for much of my life I held a single image of her, derived from the sole photograph I had seen. In it she was middle-aged and stout, standing before a shiny Ford and wearing a green felt hat with purple ostrich feathers that jutted out from the side.

But one day I saw more of her and discovered something of her exceptional history. My mother and I were sorting through old bedding and keepsakes in storage, and came upon a box of photographs of my grandmother in her twenties. All of these photos were shot outdoors, and in them my grandmother is on the move, alone or with others, restless and spirited. Laughing and shrugging, she is inexplicably pulling a donkey, itself pulling a cart, along a beach. She is gazing at a body of water too compressed to be an ocean, ready to enter. She is about to dive off a platform, cocking her head to engage the camera before she sails through the air to meet the water head-on. This last image especially supplanted her pose with the Ford. She wore the long swimming costume of the day and a bathing cap, from which her hair escaped undeterred. "She always wore a purple bathing cap, though it clashed with her red hair," my mother said with irritation. The photos were in black and white, and I couldn't see the clash.

There were also a few photographs of my grandmother with my grandfather. He is stoically poised in profile, tall and reserved in his starched collars, facial bones exquisite as a bird's. She is less fine but looks boldly at the camera. In her, evidently, nothing was held in check. They make such an odd pair that they seem posed for different photographs. As it happened, they did not fit in one marriage, and after my mother was born my grandparents split apart.

At the bottom of the box I found a long, yellowed newspaper clipping, featuring a photo of two women in bathing suits. A taller woman, dripping wet, drapes her arms over a much shorter woman and rests her head on the woman's sagging shoulder. They are exhausted, and the shorter woman's—my grandmother's—bathing cap is torn. According to the *Easthampton News,*   51 the other woman was caught in an undertow and seized with cramps. My grandmother did not hesitate to plunge into the water. The drowning woman panicked, and the two women struggled. The other woman nearly brought my grandmother down with her, until she swung her arm around the woman's chest, crushing her. She hugged the woman's body tight to her own and, though the smaller of the two, carried her through the tide to the beach.

My mother had never told me what an excellent swimmer my grandmother was. She had never shown me this clipping or told me her mother had saved a life. She said only that I had inherited my grandmother's regrettable wayward hair.

After camp ended, my sister and her boyfriend—the boy at the bottom of the tree—took me along to picnic at the lake. There were rugged trails to hike along the shore, he suggested, and boats to rent. It was late in the season, the sky unpromising, but we parked near the rental shell and spread our blanket and gear. Boats and loungers dotted the shore. My sister was irritated with me because I had begged my way into their company. She made it clear that while I could come along on the hike, I was to stay back, and I was not going out on the boat—I would have to entertain myself. We set off, Helen in hiking boots and her boyfriend with a walking stick he picked up near the beginning of the trail. I followed at a distance and was not surprised when they forgot my existence. The rain that threatened still held off, and when we came back to our blanket, Helen told me to go collect blueberries. I watched them rent a boat and saw them push off from the dock; then I went into the woods.

There were no berries this late in the year, and now a wind blew off the lake, powerful and cold. The bushes stiffened in the wind, but I paid no attention to their warning and went deeper into the thickets. Soon came the thunder, and then a heavy rain. I hurried back to the shore where we had set our things. No boat was there; they hadn't come back, though the weather had turned. Lightning opened the black sky. Through the rain and darkness I could make out no shape of my sister on the lake. I didn't know what to do. I waited; there was still no sight of them, and I cried for help. People assembled; they wondered; they ran for boats. The rain stopped, but the darkness stayed, and men headed out with flashlights and lanterns on boats. They would not take me. I stood on the shore, watching the slow circles of the swinging lights. I heard them call my sister's name, echoing across the water.

They found the boyfriend on the shore. He said my sister had stood up in the boat and lost her balance, hitting her head on the oarlock in going over the side. The boyfriend went in after her, over and over, he said. He never saw her. Her hiking boots must have weighed her down; she had tied them in a double knot on the trail. Or perhaps she was unconscious from the fall. The water was thick and black with the storm. He didn't have much strength left, and the boat was out of sight, and he swam in the direction of the lights. Late that night they found the boat bobbing weightlessly. I could not believe she did not swim to the other side and pull herself onto the banks, as she had so many times.

While we waited for my parents, I heard stories of drownings, deaths inexplicable and sudden. Everyone knew someone who had died by water. Everyone seemed to have a drowning story and to tell it. Girls disappeared in a pool of bathers, boys were trapped beneath docks. I was the only one who had lost a sister, who had been helplessly present at the drowning, although I saw nothing through the dark rains on the banks.

At school, our teacher, always dignified, tried to make the loss a part of our lesson. She drew, in language elegiac and consoling, the image of a beautiful white swan sacrificing itself to the lake and spoke of a god's thirst so deep only drowning could quench it. We sat locked in our wood seats, pulling to understand, but I could not picture the flushed face she described, the strange look of content on the body that floated to the surface. If the rescuers had found her that night, they would have hidden her face from me, for submersion quickly turns sister into stranger. But her body was never found. For me there was only an empty boat and the sound of oars knocking in their locks, and for me always a purple cap bobbing at the end of a long lake.

Now I knew the end of things before I reached them. I knew that losses pile up, and each loss bears a name. The lake's waters were not empty; she had dissolved in the lake's bottom, becoming part of its mud and history. I found that secret, anyway. I found that the features of a face can be refigured with frightening rapidity.

On every shore, whether river or lake, nearing again and again, I stumble through leaves, trample the underbrush, kick up whatever lives, forward to the edge where once in mud I believe my sister's face and body were anchored. Her drowning has anchored in my memory. If I had been allowed to go with the men on the search boats, perhaps I would have known what I cannot know—the search for my sister is fruitless. My legs pull me down to a place made familiar by loss. Each time the water is empty where once the boat lurched. I darken the water continually. What I cannot see, I cannot grasp; what I cannot grasp, I cannot break or save. I can neither see my sister, nor save her, nor break the hold she has upon my chest.

In the years after, I concentrate on this, for I alone am watching.

Ice

Christmas was so cold the water pipes froze. All the roads leading to our house were snowed shut, and we felt like fledglings in an abandoned nest—intact, but fending for ourselves in a precarious perch atop the hill. We crowded at the picture window, trying to divine movement on the horizon. Gwen's boyfriend, attempting to deliver her Christmas presents, ditched his car in a snowbank miles from our house and caught a ride on a snowplow. When the plow could cut no further, he walked, the wrapped presents piled in his arms. With binoculars my mother spotted a lonely figure trudging toward us from afar. She followed his progress, wondering how the red ribbons would fare the voyage. He remained eager, she reported, despite the obstacles. Ah love, we teased.

We were snowed in for days. Nothing moved, not in or out. Gwen's boyfriend at first couldn't believe his luck, but he eventually nurtured a secret wish that he had turned his car home. My mother was anxious about being shut in with the frozen pipes. The house felt like it was going to burst. Stabs at holiday cheer were bitter to see and hear. On the radio Judy Garland sang her mournful *Next year all our troubles will be miles away.* Our Christmas tree, dangerously tilting in its stand, was decorated a third of the way down and then petered out. The garland of glazed beads my mother had ordered as the pièce de résistance, quite lovely in the Spiegel catalog, turned out to be eighteen inches long. She'd stand at the front window for long silent periods, staring out where the road used to be, then implore my father to do something. There was nothing to be done. He stamped down the stairs to the basement in his black galoshes, checking on the condition of the frozen pipes, like a child's fever that will not break. He tapped on the pipe's casing, to little effect. Never handy under favorable conditions, he was beside himself with flustering helplessness. He'd stamp back upstairs with the dirt from the basement and snow melting into sooty puddles on the white tiles. When my mother wasn't standing at the window, she was in the kitchen arguing with him about the white tiles. He developed a fixed look, as if he saw frozen pipes everywhere. My mother scowled out at the world gone bone white. She sent me to use the facilities at our neighbors' house. I'd pee in the snow, then lick the icicles hanging from the gutters, the lamppost, and the mailbox.

On the third day I told my mother that I was going skating and set out with my skates tied together and slung over my shoulder. I wanted to lose myself in the milky stubble and took the back route through fields my mother couldn't see from the front window, down to the river, where other children gathered.

This was the river Helen had taken me to row in a blue plastic boat, when the water was deep enough. She was strong and skillful, with strokes that cut through the water clean as blade etchings on ice. One time when my paddling turned us in circles, she laughed, took the oars, and idled the boat in the middle of the river. She lifted my hand from the chipped oar and turned my child's palm skyward, to better see the vacant net of blue veins where she claimed she could see my future. She didn't say what it would be, just that I'd have one, with troubles far distant. When I thought about the future I saw myself traveling by foot on a road a long way from home, with a story to tell for each hole in my life.

We did not skate a swept pond or public rink, inlaid rounds or squares, ice evenly frozen and safe. River ice is choppy, hard to traverse. We cleared the branches, but it was never smooth. We sledded the big hills and skated the river in packs. We caught our blades and heaved into one another, pulling other skaters down with us, laughing with each pileup. We always wanted the ice to be faster. *Faster faster faster.* The river arched through the fields like a giant question mark. Bonfires glowed on the banks. Parents were elsewhere, mothers in heated kitchens, fathers in heated dens. Tiny slivers of ice floated on their windows. There were risks, and we were to encounter these alone.

At home, it wasn't a happy time of day. My mother would have trouble seeing out her window. She would be standing there, waiting for someone to return.

We had a favorite skating game. We joined hands to make a chain, swinging across the ice and throwing the last link off into the bank. We skated a certain stretch, the widest and deepest section, that curled under the stone bridge. Here we could forge the longest chain of skaters and hide if we didn't wish to be found. When the chain curled, the last skaters didn't have room on the ice and were hurled into the bank. They'd slide down on their seat to the ice, right themselves, and then skate like mad to rejoin the chain. A large, incautious dog pursued us onto the ice, barking.

Down near the stone bridge, at the deepest crossing, the ice was not solid. Ovals of water like perspiration marks pooled on top. As our chain whipped across, I fell through one of the thin patches. The other skaters edged toward shore, laughing through their brilliant red scarves. I couldn't scramble out of the hole. The water was too deep, I couldn't touch bottom, and the ice collapsed all around me. It splintered and spread out from me, and I broke through and through. Now the other skaters came off the banks, calling *M! Crawl out, M!* In the white distance, blurs of bold color. The clouds looked black and lashed together above us like ribs. The edges of the ice slid together, and the water closed over me as if I had never exploded through. Two older children and the dog inched closer, trying to calm me. The boy lay on the ice and grabbed the heels of the girl, who lay down before him and reached her hand to me, cupping her fingers so that I could cup them in mine, in a skater's chain. They pulled me onto the cracking ice, my legs splayed, snowsuit slicked to my body, my breath not quite gone.

They took me home. Nearly frozen, I walked across the alley and up the steps of the back porch to the door. It was locked, and they rang the doorbell for me. I sat down on the porch, my back to the door, facing the alley, too weak to stand while we waited. It took a long time for anyone to answer. I supposed my mother was at the front window, on the lookout. At last she opened the door, never suspecting what she'd find.

"She fell in and we saved her," the children said.

I don't know what I saw in my mother's face as I turned to her. Had she been expecting, no, hoping, for someone else to return? Did she think: another incautious daughter, this one found, this one saved, this one alive, the last link on the chain?

Only once did I see my mother lean and waver. It was on her birthday the winter of my skating accident. Fran and Gwen baked an angel food cake with pastel sprinkles and fiery candles. In tandem now, supporting the cake between them, they carried it before them like a precious, starry tiara, bending to place it before my mother.

Given the emotion of the occasion, a body that had been straight as a nail sagged. Instead of muscle and bone, the shoulders of her white blouse were bags of puffed silk, collapsing. She wept. Then she stiffened and her body never moved. She extended her neck—that linchpin—to blow out the candles, still stretching to scoff at the gods.

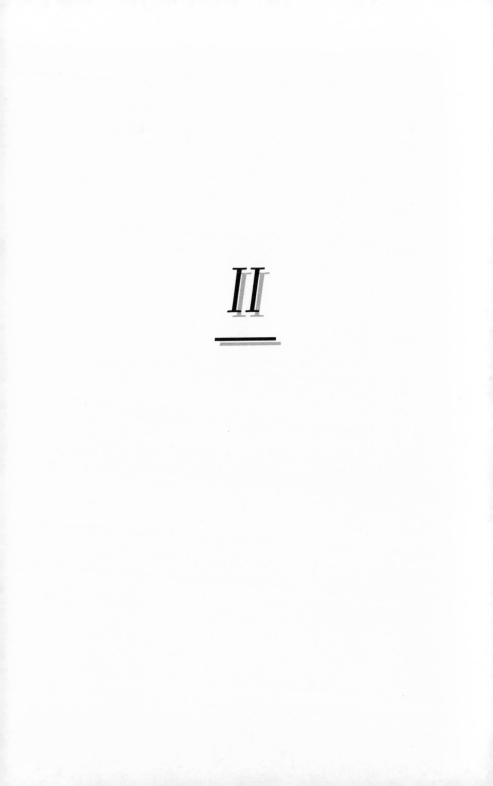

II

Girl Rearing

A new phase in my life began about this time. I began to receive a more insistent positive instruction.

Wash your hands, brush your teeth, and comb your hair. Pretend that you are in forward motion. Make your bed, fold your clothes, feed the cat, and clean the spoon. Stand up straight and pull in your stomach; don't be of unwieldy proportion, there's chocolate at the corners of your mouth. Don't bend the spine of the book or write on its pages. Your words are not better than theirs. Take your feet off the table, stop smacking your gum like a clerk at Woolworth's. Knock before entering and enter seldom. Never interrupt the flow of conversation once it's going. Napkins belong more properly in your lap, not on the floor; cats do not sleep under the bridges in Paris. Wipe your shoes before coming into the house; you may usher in messengers of doom. Learn to wait in doorways. Cross yourself before all gods, cross your legs before all men. Don't make a spectacle of yourself. Position yourself somewhere between tomorrow and yesterday. Please and thank you, I'm not your slave. You may think you are a citizen of the world, but get used to the powder room. Fingers are not used to push corn onto forks, nor should you speak with your mouth full, a fly may lay her eggs on your tongue. No joke. No stockings till ninth grade, no lipstick till eleventh, one bracelet per wrist, one earring per ear. Trees belong outside, children quiet beneath them. Peas are to be eaten by half past five. Never talk back, never say "Shut up," and never leave food on your plate, for someday you will be hungry. Waste Not, Want Not was the motto inscribed on your baby spoon. Never suck your thumb or scratch your crotch, never need anything from anyone because you won't get it. Pinch your cheeks to look like you don't live in a tent. Don't cry, don't be afraid, don't fall from trees and require medical attention. You cost a great deal and will need to pay us back and back and back. Don't be too successful either. B's are fine for girls, even C's. A's make you noticed, make you stuck-up, special. Don't overdevelop your muscles. You're too short too fat too tall too thin. What's wrong with you began before you were born, so you can see there's no fixing it. And don't entertain the idea that there is. The right man won't fix it, the perfect child won't fix it, money won't fix it, all the remedies of legend won't change the fact that you are too short too fat too tall too thin and what's wrong with you began before you were born. The question is how will you lead your life? Take the middle road, compromise, bake chicken breasts, chin-length hair, sensible shoes, a thin gold wedding band. Answer when spoken to. Never order what you really want or say what you really think or do what you really feel. Don't talk about your unhappiness or refer to divorce. Forget the past as if it never happened. Change your name if necessary. Lower your voice until it is habitually soft. You will be passed from hand to hand, it is a custom and customs never end, so travel light. Don't talk about rape, you will only make yourself suspicious. Don't hang underwear on the line. If you stand in the path of a tennis ball, you deserve to get hit. Don't pretend to be something you're not, but don't be who you are. You can never say no, nor can you really say yes. You must keep everything inside. Life is a partnership: it talks, you listen. Learn to look like you're listening. Hide your blood. Think pink.

Questions

Patsy, rumored to be the niece of Jayne Mansfield, without mother or father I ever saw, an orphan perhaps, Patsy, Patsy, my fleeting star . . .

In the spring of fifth grade, when the apple trees were blossoming and the school year was soon to end, a new girl joined the class. She appeared one day at recess. Miss Lockwood brought her out to the schoolyard, holding her hand, and walked her about for introductions. They passed from one group to the next, the children quick and thin like upright sticks, Miss Lockwood stepping crisply in her heels and sunny dress and guiding what, out of the corner of my eye, seemed to be a drifting white cloud. I was off climbing a tree, and when they reached me at last, I was hanging upside down from a branch with my dress flying over my face. The girls nearest me resumed their game of jump rope.

> My little sister, dressed in pink,
> Washed all the dishes in the sink.
> How many dishes did she break?
> One, two, three, four, five . . .

Miss Lockwood said my name, and I tucked my dress into my underpants to see.

There was Patsy—Patsy, tall but bent, big, not thin, awkward, white mohair sweater too tight despite its puffed sleeves, Patsy more substantial than any of the other girls, softer and vague, head down. Hair an unreal blond, almost white.

We were introduced, and Miss Lockwood walked away, leaving Patsy to me. Patsy leaned up against the tree, slumping there, and dragged her brand-new saddle shoe back and forth in the dust.

"Why'd you come to this school?" I asked, hanging from the branch.

She didn't answer, and I tried another approach. "Where'd you come from?"

She didn't look at me and continued to drag her shoe back and forth, making figure eights in the dust. I watched this action for a minute; it seemed familiar. "You're going to get those new shoes dirty." She looked at me but said nothing.

I hung from the branch awkwardly, watching Patsy tilting at an off-center angle, until the bell rang and we walked inside. Knees knocking together, rubbing the skin and leaving red circles, Patsy walking as if it were too much to ask of her, Patsy hardly able to carry herself into this world without her knees buckling, Patsy unable to stand straight when it was most demanded. Patsy, I liked this Patsy.

Patsy was established in a desk next to mine, with pencils and books and writing paper, and we set in to learn that plants need sun, water, and nutrients to be healthy and strong. Before that, I knew, they need dirt, holes, and dark.

Patsy didn't do well in science. She was too big for the small wood desk and chair, too big for the thin pencils that looked as if they'd snap in her fingers, too big for the lines of our composition paper from which her letters continually broke. The other girls looked small, their bodies trained to the chairs, their words pressed in place.

When Miss Lockwood asked her a question about plants and soil, Patsy whispered a featherweight sigh. Miss Lockwood could not hear her. She said, "Patsy, speak up please, I can't hear you." Miss Lockwood tried again, but Patsy pressed her lips together and uttered the same hushed sound. I thought Patsy would be good at keeping a secret.

The next day, when Miss Lockwood asked her a question, Patsy moved her lips with no sound. Miss Lockwood turned to some other child's furiously waving hand and stopped asking Patsy questions.

In art, Patsy dragged her paintbrush back and forth across the sheet of paper. She refused to turn her paintings into a recognizable shape. Told to paint our house or our mother or our dog, something or someone associated with home, some familiar image, Patsy got too much water on her brush. The paper turned soggy and heavy with indistinct, cloudy marks. Patsy's painting of home never seemed to dry, though it hung for days on a taut cord stretched across the room for everyone to see. In Patsy's pale blue painting I saw an indistinct horizon, or the open timbres of sky, its tones and colors not ours to own.

I painted what I always painted, a stick tree stuck into a thin line that wobbled across the page.

At recess the girls played skipping games.

> Two in the middle and two at the end.
> Each is a sister and each is a friend.
> A penny to save and a penny to spend.
> Two in the middle and two at the end.

If your name was called, you tried to jump into the middle while the rope whipped between the ground and air. Patsy's name was never called, but the girls asked her to be an ender. She turned the rope so feebly that it fluttered into the air like a dying bird. Then the girls didn't include Patsy in their games. I don't think she would have joined them again even if they had asked.

While the boys noticed me only to shoot me with rubber bands or to steal my crutches when I broke my leg riding my bike down the driveway with my eyes closed and running into a tree, they gave Patsy special attention. They shoved her into the library closet and kissed her. They snapped her bra. She was laughed at, stared at, joked about, and she never spoke out. I made trouble, I broke their pencils in the class and plates in the lunchroom. She never spun round and kicked the boys as I did with my cast. She never complained to Miss Lockwood of her treatment. Patsy stood alone at recess against the brick wall, unmoving, while I hung from one branch or another. Patsy of the hair flung against the rough red wall. Patsy of the soft white mohair sweater, hand raised to shield her eyes. Patsy. I spent the rest of the school year watching Patsy.

I was a little surprised when Patsy came back in the fall. I must have believed she would disperse like a mist over the long months of summer. I realized that she had a life at home, and I began to wonder what it was.

We were in Miss Joy's class. Although school had never been what I might have wished, I especially disliked Miss Joy's class.

> Here comes teacher with a great big stick.
> I wonder what I got in arithmetic.

The same lessons were taught at home.

> Tomatoes, lettuce, carrots, peas.
> Mother said you have to eat a lot of these.

A place where we were made to eat our peas and tomatoes, to finish our plates and our sentences.

I had considered the tomato and decided to shun it. I hated the way the tomato's red flesh turned pink under the cafeteria's fluorescent lights. To puncture the rubbery skin without pulverizing the mushy innards was harder than multiplication and division. I would have stood at the blackboard calculating sums through every recess, I would have stopped punching Steven Dunn in the stomach, I would have undertaken any labor to be excused from the table without finishing my tomato. One day at lunch I asked Miss Joy if I could skip the tomato on my tray.

"Rules are rules," Miss Joy said. "We make no exceptions." We were supposed to eat what we had been given, no more, no less. It didn't matter whether we liked the food or whether we were hungry.

So I ate the tomato, but not without consequences for her who made me eat it. I ate it slowly, very, very slowly. Finishing the tomato took us, that is, Miss Joy and me, beyond the lunch hour and into the afternoon. First, I inspected the tomato slices. Popping out the plentiful, hateful yellow seeds, I arranged them in a funeral pyre on my plate. After inspection began dissection, a painstaking stroking with the dull edge of my knife until the skin wrinkled and could be lifted off. I cut the slices into bite-size pieces and arranged them in rows on one side of my plate. Then I pushed the pieces to the other side to see if they'd look more edible from that angle. I decided juiciness is seldom an asset.

Finally, I had to eat the pieces of tomato, one by one, washing each bite down with gulps of milk. Swilling milk and tomatoes brought on the hiccups, from deep in the pit of my stomach. Miss Joy, annoyed, told me to hold my breath and bend over. I held it as long as I could, hiccuping all the while, and then I gasped and vomited all the milk and tomatoes. I was careful to throw up over as large an area as possible. I hit the floor, the bench, Miss Joy's shoes, and my dress, whose condition Miss Joy would have to explain to my mother.

I followed the rules, I ate my tomatoes, and I made Miss Joy sorry I had. You might say I ate my tomatoes with a vengeance.

Vengeance for myself and vengeance for Patsy. Miss Joy didn't like Patsy. She thought that she was big and awkward, that her sweater was too tight, that no one had hair so white. The power of Patsy's body was a continual shock, even though she tried to disguise it. Yet Patsy hardly touched her lunch tray and never asked for seconds. She seemed to grow on air. My mother warned me that girls must learn to push away their plates. Did someone warn Patsy as my mother warned me?

Miss Joy told her not to slump, to stand up straight. She told her that her knees knocked together. She said, "I've heard about you." She thought Patsy was dumb. I saw it differently. It's true that Patsy didn't speak up, but it wasn't that she lacked the ability, only the desire.

One day Patsy came to school with stomach cramps, and Miss Joy, annoyed, sent her to the school nurse. Patsy spent the morning in the infirmary. The nurse tried to call home, but no one answered.

When Patsy returned to the classroom, we were doing a geography game. Each of us announced our state of birth and stuck a pin in the right spot on the big map at the front of the room. There were pins clustered in Pennsylvania and a few stuck all around when it came to Patsy's turn.

Miss Joy called on her. Patsy lifted herself up and managed to get to the front of the class.

"Patsy, where were you born?" Miss Joy asked. This was interesting, because no one knew where Patsy was from. I was curious and sat up to listen. Patsy made a little sound with her lips. She was drawing her foot across the floor in front of her.

Miss Joy turned to the class. "Can you hear Patsy?" There was a little thrill in her voice. She went back to Patsy. Miss Joy made her voice sweet and girlish. "Where were you born, Patsy?" Patsy was biting her lip, but it didn't bleed, and she didn't cry. We were all watching her.

"Patsy, where were you born?" Miss Joy had dropped into her usual key. Patsy kept sweeping her shoe.

"Patsy." The voice was deep, distinct, and low. *"Where were you born?"* Patsy stood very quietly. Her eyes were looking at the windowsill at the back of the room. On it a row of potatoes sprouted in glass jars.

Miss Joy walked to the front of the room, took Patsy's hand, and led her back to her seat.

Miss Joy punished Patsy for her uncooperative silence. She made Patsy stay after school and write on the blackboard, "I will answer when spoken to." From outside, on my way to the bus,

I looked in the windows to see Patsy writing slowly, mechanically, in even rows across the board. *You should answer Miss Joy's questions,* I thought. *Do what's set out for you to do.* We were to answer when spoken to, no more, no less. But with a stick I wrote out the words *I was born in an alley* in the dust.

When the school bus had dropped me off and I was walking on the road home, I decided I would never return to school. I had no distinct plan, I just knew I was not returning.

It had rained. I did not like it to rain when I was at school, for I missed something important. Things happened in the rain I didn't want to lose. It had come down hard and continuously; leaves had been torn from the trees, and apples had fallen. I counted them as I walked.

> Mother, Mother, I am sick.
> Send for the doctor, quick, quick, quick.
> Doctor, Doctor, will I die?
> Yes, my dear, and so will I.
> How many chances will I have?
> One, two, three, four, five . . .

The apples were small, wormy, and soft. I kicked them ahead of me. Some had rolled over the sidewalk and into the road to be run over and squashed, and the pale yellow insides spilled onto the blacktop. When I lost track of how many apples, I counted and avoided cracks in the sidewalk, but not because I believed I'd break my mother's back if I stepped on one. Mothers were complete and invincible; mothers were like giants in wartime; they were beyond kissing.

Why was Patsy squeezed into clothes that were too small? Did someone think she would shrink into them? Maybe the clothes fit at the store, but by the time she got home, Patsy was too big for them. I liked that Patsy's body would fit no clothes.

The house was empty and clean. I kicked my way in the door, tracking in the moist remains of my walk. In my room the light was dim. The curtains were sewn of heavy flannel, so that no

one could see in from outside. When they were drawn, I could-
n't see out, and I felt there were no windows.

I put myself to bed and repeated, *I am not going to school for
a long time. I am going to be sick for a long, long time.* Outside
the curtains, leaves were falling in mounds beneath the trees.
Apples hung from branches like time suspended. All would
eventually fall.

> Apple on a stick,
> Five cents a lick.
> Every time I turn around
> It makes me sick.

I lay and imagined Patsy's life at home, entirely different from
school and from my own. Patsy. At home, Patsy ran up and
down, up and down, up, down the slopes in her backyard, working up an appetite. Inside for supper, she ate heaping plates of
food while laughing. After dinner, her mother fed Patsy chocolates before a fire while brushing her hair. I imagined the long,
fluid brushstrokes, the electricity of the white hair, the intimate
talk between them. *Patsy.* Her fingers were shaped and fine. The
nails shone as if the sun lit them. The hair on her arms was pale
like bits of yellow glass in the sand. *Patsy.* She lived in her mother's face, so real, so substantial, how could she paint it?

When my mother came home and found me in bed, she said,
"You've caught your chill in the rain." She brought me perfect
little cherry tomatoes and small pieces of baked chicken on a
black tray. She said, "You must make an effort to eat."

I tried to take an interest, but I couldn't. I pushed the food
away.

Then she brought toast spread with orange marmalade. This
I got all over my face.

That night I dreamed I put the food in a box under the bed.
It made an awful smell, but when the lid was shut, you could-
n't smell the rotting food. The box grew bigger and bigger. I
could feel it swelling under the bed, pushing out. It might

explode and the pulp ooze onto the floor and seep out from the mattress.

> Little Miss Pinky, dressed in blue,
> Died last night at half-past two.
> Before she died, she told me this,
> "Let the jump rope miss like this."

When I returned to school the next day, Patsy was gone. No explanation was given, and she was never mentioned again. She had never been among us. Where did she go so suddenly? I didn't know how to ask.

When I was a child, life's answers seemed to lie up ahead, beyond the last car on the hill or the bicycle disappearing in the dark. I didn't believe a tree could cause death, even an old tree like the one at the curve of the road below our house. I had been used to seeing it, leaf fused to leaf, its parts, the trunk, its lower branches, even the forsythia nearby. But I did not see the whole tree rooted beneath the sky and stars. When the speeding car crashed into it, I saw the whole tree and the yellow blossoms shaken from the branches and strewn upon the ground. The driver did not see the curve in the road. I remember nothing of her, who must have been pulled from the wreckage, and whose soft body must have lain in the grass. She was trying to get someplace fast, they said. She did not see the turn, they said. No one said, "Don't cry, sweet child." Such kindness would have baffled me, for no one had noticed that I sometimes cried.

Voice

"Children should be seen and not heard!" A woman's voice horselaughed.

I turned around to see who was talking. We had just been seated in the main dining room at the club, and words were washing over me from all the nearby tables. It was hard to tell, but I thought it was one of the blue-haired group just behind, most likely the big lady shaped like half of a large bell, who was swinging from drolleries to laughing to popping her cigarette. The words had had a smoky rasp. When the lady noticed me looking at her, I turned back to my table. My father was president of the board of officers, and as such he thought we should eat at the club at least one Saturday a month. With Fran and Gwen away at college, dinner at the club had become a more gruesome affair than before, if that was possible. I was now the only person under the age of forty in the dining room.

The waitress bustled up in her white uniform, as familiar to my family as a kindly aunt. "Good evening."

My father said, "Hello, Gertie. How are you? I think I'll have the breaded whitefish tonight."

"Breeeaaaded fiiiish," said Gertie, writing and speaking at the same speed.

"And I'll have the lamb chops," said my mother.

"Laaaamb *chops,*" said Gertie, stabbing a deep period with her pencil.

To me she said, "And you'll have creamed chicken breasts and hearts of lettuce with Thousand Island dressing. And peas." She was looking at my mother, who was nodding yes. Gertie didn't need to write it down because I always ordered the same thing; it was what my mother wanted me to eat. I had been discouraged from straying from the tried and true so many times that it was easier. It was safe.

There had been a small scene before we left the house. I had protested that I did not like the club. "There's nothing to do while we wait for the food," I argued.

My mother had said, "Waiting is something you'll be doing in life. It won't hurt you to learn how. It's a necessary part of your training." It seemed to me I had spent the better part of my life waiting for my chicken breasts. Although my mother was practiced at waiting, she too detested dinner at the club because my father exchanged pleasantries with everyone but her.

Gertie hurried off, and my father waved to two men a couple of tables away. He stood up, strolled over, and shook hands. They began to discuss the shape of the greens, a matter of great concern after the dry summer.

My right leg, which was crossed over my left leg, pumped rapidly. My mother could not see the leg under the table, but she could see my head bob along with it. She was annoyed. "Are you jacking up a car to change tires during a race?" she complained.

For many, and my parents were among the many, the thing with children was to minimize their disruption of adult life. One answer seemed to lie in silence. Children should never interfere with the flow of conversation or demand attention by speaking. These truths were enforced most at the dinner table, for this was when my family gathered under conditions that might foster talk. As a consequence my ideas about voices were mired in my ideas about food. With my sisters gone, all attention was focused on me, what I was or was not eating and how I was going about it.

The first rule at the dinner table was no talking with your mouth full. This I found most difficult to comply with since my mother and father fired questions about school at me all through the meal. If I didn't answer immediately, they became annoyed and complained I was growing unbearably sullen. I was a sad sack. If I did answer promptly, I was skewered for talking with my mouth full. Either I wasn't eating my dinner fast enough or I was *taking my own sweet time to answer a simple enough question.*

My father came back, Gertie brought the dinner rolls, and I lifted one from the basket. Then I leaned across the table and whacked off a square of butter, carrying it carefully on the tip of my large dinner knife above the candles and centerpiece back to my plate. My mother couldn't tolerate anyone who didn't use a butter knife. She went into a sort of frenzy watching this procession of the butter, the sort of horror one might feel at the sight of a man standing on the top ledge of a twelve-story building. It all seemed out of proportion to me. I couldn't understand her gasping at a single pat of butter crossing the table at 6:05 on a Saturday evening at the club.

"It is not necessary to be savage," she hissed so that the other diners would not hear. "We are civilized, you know, and would *pass* you the butter if you but asked." She wasn't through. "But no, you must lunge across the table as if we would keep the butter from you. One day a person lunges after butter, the next he steals a watch," she said with finality.

As she said this last bit, she scraped that pat of butter off my plate and returned it to where it began. Then she said in an unnaturally polite voice as stiff as plastic flowers and just as delightful, "Would you like the butter passed to you?"

She asked my father to pass the butter *please.* He passed it to her, and she passed it to me, with all the solemnity of a ritual offering to the gods. I removed that same nick of butter, but this time with my butter knife, and placed it on my butter dish. Of course, by this time the butter had melted into a small pool that could not be knifed onto a roll, particularly a roll as hard as the rolls at the club were wont to be.

I began to skulk. My mother asked, "Do you need to visit the powder room?" Here I was being quiet at the table, and still my mother was irritated. I had much to learn. Checking out the powder room occupied me through much of my girlhood.

At the club the ladies' room was called the powder room, but the men's room was called the men's room. This distinction was also part of my training, an aspect I had not yet mastered. Why was the ladies' room called the powder room? It made no sense. In all the hours I had spent there, I had not witnessed a single event involving powder.

I rose and walked by the table with blue hair and by my father and through the flood of talk and out into the quiet hallway, where the powder room was.

Even as a girl I knew this room must be approached careful-ly. If I opened the inner door unprepared, I was assaulted by a bank of mirrors, all with my own imprint. This tended to fright-en me. I had observed the most loquacious women, gabbing apace when they entered, struck dumb in the face of it.

I went through the outer door cautiously and reminded myself to look first at the vanity. I pushed through the inner door, which opened with a little whine, and there was the van-ity in front of the mirrors, with chairs pushed up underneath. On it lay a Bible and a *Ladies Home Journal* and boxes and boxes of Kleenex, one per chair. I wondered why women required such a supply of Kleenex. Maybe they needed Kleenex after catching glaring sights of themselves in the mirror.

There was no one to consult for an answer. The powder room was empty.

I didn't have much of a voice, and the one I had wasn't in demand. But as I was the sole occupant of the powder room, no one could object if I exercised it.

I looked in the mirror. The person in it didn't seem much. "You're a sad sack," I said to the mirror. The girl in the mirror was slumped over, scrunching up her diaphragm.

This conversation proceeded no further.

I sat first on one chair, then another, in front of the mirrors.

The door whined, and an older woman came through it and into the powder room. She said cheerfully, "Hello."

I said something low.

The woman said, "Speak up, dearie, I can't hear you," and turned away for a Kleenex. When she had finished with it, she left.

I thought perhaps I could practice elocution, like Julie Andrews in *My Fair Lady*. "How are you today?" I said to the girl in the mirror.

"Thank you," said the girl, "I am the same as I was yesterday. I am waiting for my chicken breasts. How about you?"

"Well, I am waiting for chicken breasts too." I tried to sound cheerful but found the effort exhausting. Julie Andrews had extraordinarily upright posture that I couldn't begin to imitate.

I tried out my voice from various locations. I walked around the corner to the stalls and stood on one of the toilet seats and spoke. Then I went to another and another to compare the differences. Then I tried bending under the doors. The differences were not impressive.

I went back to the vanity and considered the person in the mirror. I could see that she wasn't tall enough, large enough, wide enough. Her feet were too narrow to support a big voice. Her body failed her.

I believed a large body was a prerequisite for vocal power, and therefore I was attracted to the large. I liked stores catering to the Big Fellow. At the circus my favorites were the fat man and fat lady.

I envied big men and women who threw their voices around and couldn't be shouted down. I thought large people were points of emphasis in a small world. I listened to voices I admired and wondered what they ate when they were young— I was sure they didn't eat baked chicken breasts at the club. I listened intensely to records, listened to singing and felt the emotions that were forbidden in my life. I spent hours, days, years listening, hearing what I took to be the certainty and fearlessness in voices not my own.

I wanted to have a voice to glory in, a voice like Aretha Franklin's, and if I couldn't get one like hers, I'd take one like

God's, even though I hadn't heard his. Some voices floated above reality; their volume, depth, height, lushness, and extremity of utterance was not real. I figured God's voice must be good if it had parted the waters.

I looked into the mirror. "What kind of voice would you like?"

"God's, please."

At school I had written a story called "The Walk Home" and read it aloud. I raced along, running as much together as possible, hoping to get to the end quickly. To pause meant I'd hear my voice, and that was to be avoided.

At the conclusion Miss Joy said, "You raced through that one. Have you never heard of emphasis, dear? There are periods, ends of lines, paragraphs, commas, sections that are to be read with *feeling*. Slow down. Take your time. Breathe. Put yourself into it. Try it again."

This time I set a more moderate pace. Of course it still wasn't slow enough, nor was my mouth opened wide enough to make a difference. I was muttering too softly to be heard.

"You don't seem to be opening your mouth," Miss Joy was saying.

I wasn't being silent, no one could say *that*. I was speaking, but I was speaking in such a way that I didn't speak. "My dear," Miss Joy said, "you have two voices, one tentative and one too fast, and both are a misery."

Remembering this story, I knew how I disappointed, because I had been disappointing myself for a long time. If I could slow down, I would. But after a lifetime's training, how was I to slow down now?

I would give myself exercises. I would make myself read slowly, force myself to open my mouth unnaturally wide. I would work on articulation, enunciation, and projection.

I needed something to read. I picked up the *Ladies Home Journal* and glanced inside. There were pictures of Elizabeth Taylor. In one she had a big scarf tied round her head and sunglasses and round cheeks. Then in the next one she was smiling and wearing black pants that made her legs look thin. I liked the larger version. I felt disappointed when formerly large persons slimmed down. It was as if they had gone back on their word.

My mother said that Elizabeth Taylor had had a face lift. I wondered if I could get a voice lift.

I sighed and put down the magazine. I needed a voice with a more reliable size. I would try reading from the Bible. I sat down at the vanity and began paging through.

The words were hard, but I found something about God and the waters. I read it aloud: "And the dove came in to him in the evening; and, lo, in her mouth was an olive leaf pluckt off; so Noah knew that the waters were, um, abated from off the earth." The words were grand, but the voice was not. I could not feel it, nothing stirred, not in myself. I certainly wasn't going to part any water.

I read it again, slower, with emphasis, glancing up at the mirror. There was a little echo. Otherwise nothing.

I would try again, and this time I was going to concentrate, making my voice like a trumpet, like a volcano, like a ... mountain smoking. I closed my eyes for concentration and spoke with careful pace and clarity: *And the dove came in to him in the evening; and, lo, in her mouth was an olive leaf pluckt off; so Noah knew that the waters were abated from off the earth.*

I opened my eyes. A small lady in a smooth white coat was standing behind me, looking at me in the mirror with steady eyes.

The lady began to laugh. Her laugh was inconsistent with what a lady was supposed to be.

The woman kept laughing. Her laugh was not a coat to be checked. It was what it was. How would my family react if I laughed that way?

I got annoyed with the woman, who was carrying on and on. I gave her a weird look.

The woman laughed harder. It was difficult to believe she would ever stop. Her laugh built ring upon ring. There was something frightening about its intensity. There was nothing anyone could do to subdue it.

Finally the woman slowed down to a giggle, bent over to pluck a Kleenex, and wiped her eyes. I looked at her more closely. She wasn't large, though her laugh gave the impression of great size. She was hardly larger than me.

Didn't the size of her person have anything to do with the size of her voice? Her laugh rang out, but she was small. "Your laugh is big," I said, "like a *mountain*."

"Yes, I like to hear myself laugh," said the woman, poking through her purse. "It gives me hope. I love to laugh, there's nothing like it." She pulled out a pink plastic compact, flipped it open, and looked at me.

This is one strange bird, I thought.

"Anyway, what are you up to?" the woman asked. She was looking at the open Bible. She closed the compact and put it back into her purse.

Tentative, I asked her, "Do you think . . . you can change your voice? I have my doubts."

She had the compact out again. She peered at her nose in the mirror as if trying to decide whether it was a good deal.

"Well, let's take a look," the woman said. "Stand up here in front of the mirror." The woman put the compact into her purse, stood behind me, and surveyed my height and width minutely. I thought she might pull out a tape measure.

Finally the woman harrumphed and shook her head. "There are limits to what can be altered about the basic equipment. Some have been born with less powerful vocal equipment, less flexibility, less capability. These are facts." She seemed to be addressing a convention.

"But damage has been done to my voice," I said sadly, "and I'm not sure it can be put right. If you grow up eating peas and chicken breasts you can't possibly have an interesting voice. There's no nourishment in it."

"I see," said the woman. "I've eaten peas. Let me try." She picked up the Bible and read. Her voice purred. "And the dove came in . . ."

Her voice had currents that ran along like the runs of a trout stream, and it pooled, gathering force and glory. More than anything else, there was force.

The voice did not spare me. The woman had suffered for that voice and in that voice. It was dirty with disappointment, with floods and flat tires and broken glass and fishhooks and slammed screen doors. The gravel of roads that led nowhere. Neon signs flashed with only half the letters lit.

I wiped my eyes with a Kleenex. As I looked at my small figure in the mirror, I wondered if I gained weight whether my voice would gain that sort of power. Maybe its volume would increase. I might be heard from blocks away.

"Maybe my voice would be more interesting if I got bigger."

"Well, I'm sure you will grow bigger, dear. There is no doubt about that," the woman said, smiling sweetly.

"No, I mean much bigger."

"Oh, you hope that its tones will be deeper, fulsome and irrefutable. You want a resplendent voice birds can build nests in, a voice of unearthly beauty on an operatic scale." The woman was getting herself worked up again. "What you really mean," she said, looking at me almost angrily, "is that maybe you will have a say in things more often, and what you say will be taken seriously."

"*Yes*. That's what I want!" I was certain I would be heard if only I had such a voice.

"You are wrong," said the woman, "dead wrong."

The woman was fumbling with her compact. "You know it's been said, 'Thoughts that come on dove's feet guide the world.' What you really need—darn!—is to hear the voice you have been given, a voice of ordinary proportions to be sure. How can you change it if you cannot hear it?"

"I want to hear my voice," I said. "I really do."

She looked at me. "You have a voice that is better than it sounds. It may take you most of your life to realize it."

I had looked in all the wrong places.

"I have something to tell you. Close your eyes."

I did as I was told.

"You must concentrate and be very still. Are you ready?"
I nodded.

The woman whispered in my ear: "Now listen very carefully. Listen to the voice of someone who cares for you." I waited, concentrating and being very still. I was tense, and then more relaxed. I waited, trying to relax.

I thought of Toni, who babysat and ironed for my mother. The ironing room was downstairs, out of the flow of traffic in the house. Sometimes she turned on the radio and sang along. Sometimes she sang "Somewhere over the Rainbow." She had a tremulous voice like a bird's. Toni sang while she pressed rumpled cloth into shirts. I thought about its existence, that I heard singing in the house, the only live voice I heard sing in my house. I would go into the room next to the ironing room quietly, so as not to disturb her. She would have stopped had she known I was there. It seemed that Toni was singing to me from the other side of the powder room wall.

I woke from my reverie. I opened my eyes. The powder room was empty.

I wandered back to my table. My mother and father were eating. "What have you been doing all this time?" my mother asked.

I sat down and began to eat my chicken breasts.

I pretended I was singing. Some potential was secreted away in my voice. It was not my skin, which could never come off. It came from deep inside me and pooled at the back of my mouth. My voice came as a surprise, deeper, richer, more certain, even powerful. I paused. I slowed down and sped up. I was flexible, I sang with emphasis. I opened my mouth and sang.

I yawned. I felt complete. The room was peaceful with the dry chinking of knives, forks, and plates. I felt full of different, powerful feelings. Sometimes sadness, but not always. Sometimes the sadness was the realization of all I hadn't been feeling.

"Napkins belong in your lap, M. *M!* Napkin in your lap!"

Kitchen

My mother would have liked to tell this story:

> In the beginning of the world, there was a kitchen
> with a woman standing in it, looking forlorn. All
> around the dark kitchen the world shone radiantly.
> And some voice said, "Let there be dinner." Not *food,*
> mind you, dinner. So evening came, and morning
> came, and it was the same thing, and it was called
> domestic life.

Of course my mother did not tell this story and could not tell it.
Had she told it, I would not have understood, and I would have
looked perplexed. Then she would have peered intently at me,
and her brows would have contracted until her eyes turned
hard. "From the kitchen," she would insist, "the sun cannot be
seen."

My mother did not speak lyrically of orange tarts and trout.
She did not regard the preparation of food as a central source
of meaning. Baking was not the last stage in her education. She
did not want to be buried in the concrete, up to her elbows in
flour and grease. Perhaps if she could prepare a timeless meal
that we would sit down to eternally but never touch, if the family could remain frozen in admiration, perhaps cooking would
be worth it.

Food was not a forbidden pleasure for my mother. She was
not one who ate moderately in public view and then gorged
when thought to be washing the dishes. She had no secret cache

of chocolates. She did not speak the language of dieting because she was above the banality of binge and purge. She never binged, and there was no need for repentance. She ate moderately at all times. Holidays did not affect her. She could not be tempted to seconds. Even better than being satisfied with one roll was to leave the roll half-eaten, to remind all of the self-control we lacked but she possessed. She insisted on small portions in neat triangles on her plate. The food was never allowed to mix and mingle—to slop, as it were. Peas stayed in their pyramid, while the chop kept its central place on the plate.

One might assume that keeping such tight rein on herself would occupy all my mother's energies. But no, I too had to maintain order upon my plate and grow accustomed to small portions and restrained appetite. It was a family value never to speak of hunger or want more food than one was given. My mother stormed when someone used up the butter. It was better to go hungry than to finish the jam. My mother purchased one quart of ice cream to last two weeks. On alternate weeks, she would allow the family to simply look at the ice cream in the freezer and think about dessert. The thinking about would be as good as the having, she'd reassure, and further, the having would be better for the not having. Returning home from some errand, night out, or vacation, my mother inspected the ice cream to verify its condition. Under her management, a quart of ice cream lasted a whole month.

But sometimes a babysitter liked ice cream. Toni *loved* ice cream. Sometimes to console herself for the task of staying with me or other good reasons in her own difficult life, Toni ate a big dish of ice cream. Perhaps she calculated my mother would not notice for a few days, being tired after a late evening, or what with the fluster of settling back into normal life after a vacation. Little did Toni know that the first thing my mother did was evaluate the freezer. Sometimes she had eaten what my mother denounced as vast quantities of ice cream. At the time I believed she ate what my mother said—an unbecoming amount. Only after having myself eaten what legitimately could be

called vast and unbecoming quantities of ice cream did I realize what Toni actually consumed.

What really floored my mother was when Toni left three
spoonfuls of ice cream in the bottom corners of the container.
This stratagem was curious to me. Was the fear of finishing food
so powerful that even Toni was not free of it? Did Toni think
that the full absence of the container of ice cream would be
dealt with severely? When she returned from Antigua or
Bermuda or Jamaica, my mother's vacation was undone by the
three remaining spoonfuls.

My mother hated to spend money on the kitchen. She never
bought the new gadgets. She liked to show me a shiny vegetable
peeler given her when she was first married. Sometimes she
brought out all the utensils from the early days and proudly displayed them. They looked small and mysterious on the coun-
tertop.

She thought kitchens a waste of perfectly good space. My
parents engaged in one home improvement project after another, and few areas were untouched—except the kitchen. An
upgraded kitchen would demand a parallel improvement in my
mother's cooking. She would rather *shrink* the kitchen. When
my parents were looking at houses before moving to Twenty-
second Street, she dumbfounded the real-estate agents by seeking smaller and smaller kitchens. She hoped that in old age
there would be none at all, and she would be relieved of cooking at last.

Our kitchen was a lonely place, unenlivened by a single plant
or windowsill herb. We had the smallest refrigerator money
could buy, and it verged on emptiness—a smidgen of butter on
a plate, a shriveled apple, a disappointed box of baking soda,
some ice trays crackling in the freezer. The cabinets weren't
much better. No bags of flours and sugars or containers brim-
ming with pastas. No telltale baker's dust on the shelves. No
cookie jar or breadbox on the counter; no rack of spices, no lazy
Susan spinning with cinnamon and cayenne, no dried beans.
One might find a half-eaten box of crackers, the remainder dead

stale, or stained packets of Lipton's Cup-of-Soup. My mother liked to point out that "few emergencies require large amounts of navy bean soup." And it was true. On just one occasion were we snowbound, and we didn't eat any navy bean soup.

My mother preferred processed food, what she called boxed dinners. A good meal, in her view, came out of a small box, went into the oven, was nibbled at and thrown away. She did not venture from a list of bland favorites because she liked to "control the variables." I did not quite understand this, but I knew my mother's stance toward food was not adventuresome.

Cooking and eating were inextricably linked, so my mother impeded all processes associated with either. She fought on all fronts. She never had enough coffee mugs to drink from or silverware to eat with or chairs to sit on. In this way she severely limited her family's access to food. There were no sieves, no pie or cake pans, no rolling pin or cookie cutters, only a partial set of measuring cups. Appliances were kept in need of repair. The can opener would cut a few degrees of arc and quit. My mother was forced to tear the lid out, nicking her fingers.

The trash can was the pièce de résistance, the most perfect embodiment of denial. It was quite beautiful, hand-painted metal in black, tan, and cerulean blue. Its lid was a larger version of the kind on holiday cookie tins that require two hands and fortitude to pry off. Because of the occasional nature of holiday cookie tins, the lid can be lived with. But many times in the course of an ordinary day my mother had to put something in the trash. Each time she would brace her foot against the lower portion of the can and pull with all her strength to break loose the vacuum-sealed cover. Inside, a small bag was revealed, smaller than a shopping bag—for the can was small. Its limited capacity resulted in regular overflow and frequent changes, all to be executed by my mother in despair. When I suggested acquiring a new, larger, more convenient trash can, I was met with fury. "This one is just fine, thank you," my mother said. "I won't spend another penny on this kitchen."

She gave disquisitions on buying habits. "Some women,"

she'd say, "don't have room for the groceries they buy. That's a fact. Columns of toilet paper stacked to the ceiling in bathrooms, making movement very difficult; drawers overflowing with soaps, deodorants, air fresheners, toilet bowl cleansers. Some women look for 'specials' the way children look for shiny pennies. They clip coupons and spend their days driving from store to store buying products they believe are worth more than the sales price. Sales beget a sales mentality. I don't like reduced goods." Not only did she never clip coupons, chase sales, or purchase in bulk, she selected only the smallest size. Picnic jars of mustard, mayonnaise, jam, pickles. A pint of milk, snack-size chips and pretzels, the tiniest cans of tuna, one roll of toilet paper. Napkins she would not purchase, for they came in packets of forty.

She could not bring herself to plan the week's meals and make a list of the required groceries. She put off shopping and put it off, thinking she could nap now, act later. She couldn't face the reality of the seven dinners ahead. Dinner, the question of it, pervaded her life. My mother would ask me wistfully, "Why must days end with a substantial meal? It takes hours to prepare and nearly as long to clean up. Why can't the day end as it began, with a piece of toast?"

I saw that the answer to her question was marriage. My mother was in charge of the kitchen. It was her domain, and out of its depths dinner was supposed to appear on a nightly basis.

My father said that that was the deal. He explained, "Dinner is the one thing I expect of your mother, and it is the one thing she won't do. I don't expect her to clean the house or iron my shirts; we pay Toni to do that. And I don't expect her to pay the bills or make my lunch. I don't expect her to do anything at all except prepare dinner and have that dinner ready sometime fairly soon after I arrive home. I don't even expect her to prepare meals I especially like. It isn't much, but she won't do it."

A woman who hated to think about food, my mother spent more time shopping than women who love nothing better than filling their carts to the brim. It was not uncommon for us to make several trips to the store to complete a single dish, for she never wrote down all the necessary ingredients, and she never had anything on hand. Dinner was supposed to be served at precisely six o'clock, never a shade earlier or later. Not the sophisticated hour of seven or the plain hour of five, but at six o'clock, the ineffabably modest hour of the in-between. My father arrived home at five-thirty sharp and had just enough time to inquire what we were eating, nod, and retire to his overstuffed chair in the living room for a quick perusal of the newspaper before his chin collapsed onto his chest. As the big hand on the grandfather clock struck six, the two heads above its face shifted positions and blushed in passing. My father jolted up from his recliner as if to dispel any impression that he was dozing. But he was able to nod off again, for at seven o'clock, eight, my mother was still to be heard in the kitchen, banging pots, making dinner.

I told my mother to cook large quantities and freeze some for another week. I told my mother to cook food nobody liked, so as to create leftovers. I was telling her to rethink food and dinner and her relation to it, that is, to change her life. But my mother did not do any of these things.

As for me, it would have been safer, and certainly more economical, had I learned a few basics in kitchen management. Better to have known how to turn things on and off, to read and follow directions, to deflect crisis even when I seemed programmed to create it.

In eighth grade, in the dead of winter, the day before my mother's birthday and three days before my own, I got the idea to make her something to eat—as a surprise. I wanted to repay my mother for a kindness, and I wanted to liven up her winter.

My mother had an evening charity meeting and was gone from the house. My father withdrew to the living room to read about the wide world in the newspaper. He might as well have been in Africa. Searching the shelves for something to make, I found Jell-O, orange Jell-O. I was glad to spot it because there wasn't much on our shelves, and we didn't own cake pans or a mixer. The classic *Betty Crocker Cookbook* tells us that molded salads, that is, Jell-O with something imprisoned within, are the preferred way women express themselves. Plus, as any experienced adult knows, Jell-O is one of the easiest things to make. Surely I can do it, I thought.

But following directions on the box seems to be a prerequisite for success, and keeping track of the time is another—neither of which I did. With the knack of the savage, I neglected to add water to the mix. I just poured the contents into the pot, put on the lid, and turned on the burner. I suppose I assumed that the powder would melt when heated, becoming the liquid I had seen my mother stirring once when she made Jell-O.

I went to my room and did my homework. I became engrossed in Egyptian pyramids and forgot about my mother.

Suffice it to say, a surprise did greet my mother upon her return, but it didn't make her birthday the entirely happy event she had hoped for. I set the burner on fire, which is to say there was a fire in the kitchen and I started it—although it has remained a mystery how dry Jell-O in an aluminum pot can start a fire. The house filled with smoke. This was before smoke detectors, and it must be a monument to my father's and my dedication to higher things that we did not notice until the house had darkened with smoke at our separate ends. The top of the stove was destroyed, and the wallpaper was blackened in all the front rooms.

My mother seemed as angry with my father as with me; it was hard to distinguish the degrees of rage in the far-reaching heavens of her anger. But finally she was angrier with me because I had made her angry with him. "Clearly I have failed in my maternal duty," she announced to the kitchen, wiping the residue of wreckage from several appliances, "for I have produced a daughter even more incompetent than I." She did seem truly astonished. She looked at me as if I might be replaced.

From then on, I was not allowed in the kitchen except to deposit my dirty dishes. I wasn't allowed to run the dishwasher or wash my own clothes. My mother didn't want me to come in near proximity to an appliance, as if my body could launch anarchy.

The singed smell, which might deter anyone from an intimacy with Jell-O, seemed to hang in the house for months, to affect our noses whenever my mother and I sniffed at each other. Even now, when I imagine the Jell-O incident might at last be behind me, a whiff of what defies description, an odor of the wild, accidental, and nameless, oftentimes rises up from some corner it has settled in.

Uncle

My father's brothers were all medical men—doctors of the
eyes, ears, nose, throat, and teeth. I saw them at yearly check-
ups or on holidays, unlikely times to get to know relatives, and
I did not know them well. They didn't have much to say to me,
except for Uncle James, who was my dentist and wore a brilliant white smock. Though not particularly tall, he had a high-
stepping physique, like a sandpiper, with long, stiff legs that he
picked up gingerly and carefully set down, avoiding obstacles.
Entering our house for holiday visits, Uncle James would look
in the big picture window with trepidation, craned on his long
legs at the window lit with wedded drama. At family gatherings
he skipped the adults and sat cross-legged on the floor with a
ring of children, joking and gaming. At Christmas he lavished
presents of drum sets and trampolines. It was on the trampoline
Uncle James gave me that I performed my first flip.

Uncle James was called an eligible bachelor, unmarried and
well employed. But in truth he was ineligible. I never saw him
with any woman but his dental assistant or his arthritic mother, my grandmother, with whom he lived and to whom he was
devoted. He was rumored to have once eloped with a voluptuous redhead to Atlantic City and to have had the marriage
annulled before anyone found out. I could picture the redhead—
she had exquisitely polished nails with matching patent leather
bag and shoes, and her hair flamed out against a daring dark
dress—but I could not see Uncle James anywhere near her. It was
not a topic agreed upon for conversation in the family, even

decades after the marriage was supposed to have happened that the family denied had occurred. My father was once asked about it by a golf partner at the club. He stepped off the tee, saying gravely, "I will not set foot on this course with you." In fact, he never played golf again, but it didn't matter because he had lost his swing anyway.

At the reception after Gwen's wedding, Uncle James and I found safety together in a doorway. Neither of us was in a joking mood. I was a flower girl, terribly uncomfortable in the stockings and garter belt I had donned for the first time.

Looking over the crowd dappled with friends of the bride, Uncle James mused, "They'll all marry sooner or later. More probably sooner than later. Even the best of them become wives in the fullness of time. Look at your sisters."

I glanced around the room. Women stood in rings ever circling, circling, men with their backs to the fire, nursing scotch and talking about the club.

"I dislike wives in fur coats more than anything," Uncle James said, "especially standing in doorways. So hard to pass, you know."

His life lay outside the intrigues of marital bliss. This location did not seem to sadden him.

"Many marry against their better judgment," he said. "Love has nothing to do with a decision to marry, or it shouldn't. But that's the common mistake. We put the question of marriage in such a way—do I love?—that loads the dice. The answer to the question—do I love?—is not the same as yes I want to be married. The world demands that we marry to go on loving, and since most of us don't want to live a life without love, we comply."

He did not like to step into the middle of things. He stepped over patches of ice in winter and over puddles of mud in the spring. He didn't seem to like having his feet touch the ground. I pictured Uncle James on his high stiff legs trying to step over matrimony, using all the ingenuity in his long legs to scurry by women standing in solicitous rings.

"An old story," he was saying, "the woman who loves, the

man who loves, both thinking that marriage will give shape to what they feel. Marriage is supposed to clear the way of every impediment to love, but if it's safe, is it still love? There is no such thing as safe love. It's a malocclusion. It can make you weep."

Uncle James never referred to an unfortunate early marriage to a redhead, though he liked redheaded children. "When women mature," he once said, "hair with sunbursts is no longer appropriate." He also avoided passing through New Jersey. "Of New Jersey," he said, "I will have none." Uncle James made pronouncements about women and geography, often in conjunction.

On weekends in the summer Uncle James traveled to his shore house, ramshackle, sunlit, with peeling paint, built right down to the beach. There he liked to paint watercolors of the fishing boats and sea life. When I was little, he sometimes took me along. When we had finished breakfast, he'd scoop me from the table, put me on his shoulder, and carry me to the shore. He'd wade right into the surf and toss me as if I were a beach ball, laughing, crossing back and forth above and through the waves. I was turned like a jewel on a bracelet. At the shore, Uncle James was no longer cautious or craned, no longer stiff and high stepping. Here he liked to be in the middle of things, his arms and legs jumbled in the rising swell and ocean spray.

Uncle James wanted to bypass wives standing in their solicitous rings, step over them or around them. Yet they were like snowdrifts that blew across his path. Safest was his bachelor life at the shore, divorced from his professional and family life at home. He separated his life into discrete piles, like loads of laundry—the socks from the shirts, cottons from polyester, stark whites from the darks, which bled and bled and bled.

Ingenuity

I lay awake at night and thought of horses: horses on the horizon, grazing arc in black composure, a crease of fireflies, a riddle bunched close, the soft shuffle of hooves down the hills, rhythmic thought gathering in, drumming on my arid girlhood.

It seems to have existed from the beginning, so that it could not end. The wildness of horses pulled at me. I longed to touch a horse, and for horses to touch me. I did not want to play or pretend: the figurines my parents bought in gift shops bored me, and as for horse stories, I could not endure the terrible tale of *The Red Pony* or *Black Beauty,* the blessing given and then torn away, ungiven. But there were pony rides at the fairgrounds with my father, and soon I was appealing for riding lessons. My mother resisted, arguing that horses were dirty, dark, and dangerous (this I knew or had dreamed), and I was forced to limp instead through piano and ballet. Fortunately for my hopes, my mother finally grasped the futility of further efforts in that direction; she yielded, and I was allowed to begin weekly lessons.

Scouting about for riding instructors, my parents chose a newcomer to town, Miss Reba, probably because she was willing to ferry some of us to the stable in her station wagon on Saturday mornings. When she arrived to pick me up, I discovered that she looked like Jackie Kennedy. There was a resemblance in size, build, and coloring, and in something else I could not name, complicated eyes that saw the beginning and the end at once. It was not a resemblance in style or carriage. Miss Reba was a tougher, more muscled version, and she made other women seem soft and unreliable, as if they couldn't be counted on in a jam.

Miss Reba knew the meaning of *hurry*. As we waited at a red light, she turned around and, fixing a dark eye on us, asked, "So what have you heard about me?" No one was that direct, and we all inspected the shine on our new boots. She was already teaching before we arrived at the stable. As she hit the gas and passed a slow truck, she said, "You'll learn that people don't approve of girls riding horses. It's all right when you're small, but later they call you promiscuous or unfeminine."

Promiscuous, what did it mean? And what did it have to do with riding horses?

"I'm not interested in how pretty you look on a horse," she continued. "I'll teach you to ride so that you feel the wind and see the shaking ground, but there might not be a horse under you." She laughed. "All that will take a while." We shifted in the backseat uncomfortably. What kind of riding was this? It was the last thing we wanted to hear before we had ever mounted a horse.

Her stable was out of the way, approached only by dirt road, and a little rundown. She lived on the premises in a trailer parked up the hill from the main barn. The property was large, with trails winding through the wooded areas that spread away from the barn and riding ring. The trees just around the ring had by the neglect of the previous owner become overgrown and unwieldy, but in the hot days of summer they provided cooling shade for the horses. One of Miss Reba's first acts of ownership was to hang a sign bearing the name of the stable near the gated entrance from the dirt road, though the trees obscured it. She called her stable the Black and Blue, as a little joke, and underneath, inscribed in small letters, were words in French, *L'espoir luit comme un brin de paille dans l'étable.*

"What does it mean?" I asked Miss Reba.

"Hope shines like a wisp of straw in a stable," she said.

Around horses Miss Reba was all business; she tolerated no nonsense, silliness, or cowardice. "Horseback riding isn't being hoisted into the saddle and galloping away," she told us. "It takes years before anyone belongs on a horse." She showed us the mounting block, a chunk of cement with relief figures of stable boys, which stood just outside the barn. "Riding includes mounting and dismounting. Some people use these when they're starting out. We're not going to use one. Some people have a stable hand to lift them into the saddle. We're going to learn to mount our horses ourselves." If this caused difficulty, even pain, so be it. "Riding isn't playing with dolls. Horses aren't small pieces of plastic. If you want to play with dolls," she said, picking up a handful of dust and dribbling it through her fingers, "they aren't here."

There were girls younger than I and girls older. Some of the youngest spent the first session trying to get up on the horse. Some girls managed to mount but couldn't move out of the stable to the riding ring. If our horses didn't want to budge from the shelter, it was our job to move them, but we were forbidden to use a crop or to kick a horse. "Ingenuity is required," Miss Reba reminded us, leaning against the barn door and smoking a cigarette. "If you got your parents to allow you to take riding lessons with me, you can get your horse to move. They aren't nearly as obstinate." I studied my horse, Old Jones, and judged the obstinacy between him and my mother too close to call. But he stood still as a statue as I tried to climb up his sides and fell off a few times, and finally I was able to settle into the saddle.

Girls who got their horses moving rode slowly down the lane toward the ring, wearing expressions of grim triumph. I was one of these. My departure from the stable, however, was not immediately succeeded by my arriving ringside, for my mount stopped at a tree to munch leaves. From my high post I could watch a couple of the more advanced riders shuffling round the ring, and I marveled at their achievement. I flailed at the reins to jerk Old Jones's head out of the tree. My efforts fell on his neck as a light summer rain, and my supply of ingenuity almost

dried up. Afraid the lesson would end right there, I dismount-
ed—the last resort, it had taken so long to get up—grabbed the
reins, and pulled, and I mean pulled him down to the ring,
where I climbed the fence and jumped back on. Miss Reba
seemed to accept this launching pad, and I was able to enter the
circle. Thus ended my first day as a rider.

As our lessons went on, we improved at moving from the stable to the riding ring, but what happened once we got there was
not in our control. We tried to hug the outer rail, but no one
made a horse do what he didn't want to do. If you were lucky,
he wanted to do what you had in mind. Oftentimes the horses
appeared unaware of our presence. They wandered into the center and came to a halt, or they rubbed up against the fence to
eat the grass that grew from the other side. With our mounts at
a standstill, we tried to look like real riders—we kept our heads
low and our chins tucked in, as Miss Reba was teaching us to
do.

Miss Reba planted herself in the center of the ring, always
holding a cigarette, and called out instructions. Keeping steady,
controlling the body to work with the horse, was at the heart of
her teaching. "Control yourself, not the horse," she would say.
"Heels and hands down. Toes point in, legs hug the horse all the
way down, and I don't want to see daylight between the saddle
and you." We walked our mounts about the outer circle, squeezing our knees tight, keeping our heels and hands down, trying
not to bounce or flounce or fall backward or fall forward onto
the horse's neck. When there was control, it came by moving
with the horse through invisible leanings and squeezes.
Advancing from a walk to a trot, we were told, "Urge your horse
forward and faster by pressure originating from your seat.
Incline forward, apply more pressure, move your hands slightly up the horse's neck. Do not fall forward or support yourself
on the horse's neck. Keep the body still and hunkered down in
the saddle."

Her praise was rare and terse; she was more likely to blame.
Disgusted sometimes at my clumsiness, Miss Reba would pinch

out her cigarette and stalk out of the center, snapping, "Bad riders show *everything*. They jerk up their horses' heads, hold the reins clutched too tightly on the horses' neck. Look as if you're just sitting on the horse's back and going along for the ride, M. No one should see the effort. Ride as if you're not riding."

The months passed, and our muscles began to develop without constraint. My parents noted a transformation. As I came up the walk from the driveway to the front door, they smelled it. They saw it in the callouses on my hands when I opened the door, heard it in the heavy thud of my boots up the stairs.

Over dinner one night my mother lamented, "How sad it makes me to see your pinky fingers permanently bent. I wonder that I didn't listen to what people told me about her."

"What did they tell you?"

"She's too . . . detached. Never mind." She stared at my face, in which rough dirt and sweat surpassed all scrubbing. "You even walk strangely." She was right. Like a sailor, a rider remains herself, regardless of the element below. It was this that I had seen in Miss Reba's carriage from the beginning.

Yet I never saw her on a horse. A girl once asked her, "Why don't you ever ride?"

"I do ride," she answered. "But not on a horse."

"How can you ride without a horse?"

She laughed. "It takes ingenuity."

In my second year I was able to move outside the riding ring to follow the trails through the surrounding woods and fields, on Old Jones or Tom Thumb or one of the other lesson horses. I was spending a weekday afternoon at the stable in addition to my Saturday lessons, then two afternoons, then as much time as my parents would allow. Jones and Tom Thumb were better known to me than my family. I brought them carrots and apples and rode the ring and followed the trails endlessly. Miss Reba's stable was different from others. At the Black and Blue you had to learn how to keep a horse, muck out stalls, feed, groom, clean tack, mend fences, back a horse into a trailer, fix a shoe. The Black and Blue became my home, or a world apart from my home, with different lessons to teach me about girlhood. In this I was not alone. Parents dropped their daughters off at the entrance to the stable near the sign Miss Reba had hung, foregoing the dirt road up to the main barn as if they were not welcome to enter. In our gear we trudged together up the lane like a squad of foot soldiers, dusty before we arrived at the barn, anything but the prim daughters we were elsewhere training to be.

Somehow Miss Reba herself stayed clean amid the muck of the stable, defying Mrs. Galloway's law. She often wore a white button-down shirt, freshly ironed, tucked into tan breeches, with the sleeves rolled halfway up and the top buttons open. Sometimes, when she was going out that night, her hair was hooked up in uncanny giant rollers under a bright scarf, as if the usual human preparations were insufficient. This, like everything else about her, was mysteriously wonderful to me. I told her that I loved the horses, their dark beauty, the smell of them. I could not be near them enough.

"What's happening with you is what happens," Miss Reba said. "You start with a desire for contact with horses. You begin to learn how to ride, to belong on a horse, and to love them." She smiled a little, then said, "But you always want something more than what you have."

In the fall of my third year Miss Reba called me over one afternoon and looked at me for a minute, silently. Then she said, "I'm acquiring a new horse for the stable, a thoroughbred who's never been ridden. He's going to learn to jump. Maybe you would like to ride him and help take care of him and learn to jump with him."

"Oh yes, oh *yes*."

Miss Reba warned me that he would require as much care in grooming and feeding as a baby and considerably more exercise. I would be the first person to get on his back, the first to put a bridle in his mouth, to saddle him, to ride him. She had decided that I was ready to take the responsibility, and she told me, to my amazement, that my mother had agreed.

I first saw him on my thirteenth birthday. My parents drove me through the snow to the stable. A brass plate on his stall door read ALERT INDIAN in large letters. When Miss Reba opened his stall, snow was falling outside the window behind him, and the straw was fresh and golden and piled thickly. Standing in the straw was sixteen hands of blackness. When the door slid open, every inch of him was startled. His muscles tensed from his head all along his back to the flicking tail. His neck was arched and tight, his eyes widened and white, his head high and turned toward me. It was finely shaped, intelligent, watchful. His muzzle was a soft, smooth black. He exceeded my thought of what a horse could be.

In the beginning I didn't ride him. I stood outside his stall and stroked his neck through the bars if he'd let me, feeding him carrots and apples, then moving inside. I studied him, and he studied me. Eventually I led him out of the stall by the halter, and I walked him. I let him out to pasture, and I brought him in. Sometimes he came on his own when he saw me sitting on the top rail of the fence.

I had a living thing for whom my voice mattered, someone to be steady for. I had to be steady. Horses hear and feel intensely; they do not minimize danger. They enlarge where we reduce. Alert was easily spooked on the periphery of his vision—a wind blowing leaves in the lane, or a sudden sound, a car starting. If I frightened Alert, he was gone, withdrawn into a world of his own. I spoke softly to him. I tried to become an acceptable part of his world. I learned to move quietly. He might, I thought, even look forward to my touch.

After weeks of preparation, Miss Reba said it was time to try the saddle. A young horse does not simply accept a bit in his mouth, the cold silver on his gums. Inside a horse's mouth are rose petals. A young horse does not accept a saddle on his back, the tightened girth. He fights.

At last it was time to ride, and Miss Reba said to take it lightly. Alert was the most beautiful of horses, but fragile. His front legs turned slightly out at what we think of as the ankle, and his weight tended to shift to the inside of the leg, its weakest part. Miss Reba said I must not break Alert, but fall in with him. When I lifted myself into the saddle for the first time, Alert was startled to find that I should do it. He twisted to one side and another, trying to shake me loose. I let him shy away from me, let him shake me loose. Miss Reba had taught me that you must let a horse resist your riding. I climbed back onto Alert and tried again. He shook me off, and then he shook me off again. But then we found that he was walking with me, not shaking me off. We walked the riding ring, then moved out onto the trails, always walking.

Then I was able to let him run. I cannot say what this running was to me, freedom, power, and speed like nothing else, together with Alert.

Miss Reba sometimes told me I was doing well. "Now you're ready to learn that riding is a way of being with the horse where there is no control," she said. "When you really ride there is nothing different from yourself to control. The horse and you move together, like one thing." Alert and I moved together—or that was my intent. When we did not, I fell off, having gone one way when Alert went another. Sometimes he went over the jump without me, or I went over without him. But I, who was impatient with most tasks and most people, was never impatient with him. For Miss Reba counseled patience.

"Riding is just the beginning of riding," she told me.

"What do you mean?"

"You see there's falling, too." She laughed a little. "And other things."

We began to ride in horse shows, jumping events in which falling off and getting back on were expected occurrences. We hardly went home. My parents attended a few shows and then stopped coming. It frightened my mother to see the risks I took with perfect composure. In truth I never felt the bruises until hours later.

Miss Reba's lessons went on. "Riding is in the hands. You and Alert talk through the hands," and I was to keep my hands quiet.

"Ride with a long hold, reins loose, almost loopy. Horses don't respond to riders making busy demands upon them. The reins tell him what he needs to know. And he tells you. Does he want you to pull him in or let him go, does he like a shorter rein or a longer, hands on or off his neck?"

But then other times she said, "Imagine you don't have hands. Imagine there's no horse there." And sometimes there *was* no horse there. I often fell, and Alert would saunter over to where I lay, looking at me quizzically: What are you doing on the ground?

When I caught Alert's rhythm, I found that it was mine, the music I was yearning for. The reins fell loose in my hands, looser, till they disappeared; I did not need them. The fast ground shook below me till it vanished, and I was not myself but a movement over the face of the world, a blessing. I rode every day, and every day became riding, and riding became inseparable from Alert. I did not want to get on another horse, ever.

I told Miss Reba, "With a horse you have to start at the beginning. Alert hasn't spent his days walking in circles. He's loyal to me. He even stands still for me to groom him—you don't have to tie him up like the other horses."

Miss Reba said, "That's good, M., because riding isn't controlling. When you and Alert go over a jump together, there's no control. I've seen what can happen when you try to pull a horse over a jump. You're like Alert's skin. When he jumps, you jump."

So I progressed in my apprenticeship, on the crunching pasture of winter, the dry grass of summer, the spongy turf of spring and fall, and in a circle I thought could never end.

In winter, when the ground turned hard, exercise was a difficulty for Alert because of his stride. Miss Reba told me to walk him on a lead or, if it seemed safe, to ride him lightly. One day, in our fourth winter together, I woke to find the limbs of the trees stiff in the wind of a snowstorm. The ground was icy hard, and I phoned Miss Reba to tell her that I did not think I would be able to come to the stable because of the storm. That afternoon one of the stable hands let Alert out to pasture, and when he came back to the barn, he was limping. X-rays showed that he had broken the navicular, a small bone deep in the hoof.

Alert was now severely restricted; our jumping ended. He wore special shoes to counteract his inclination to lean in. We followed a strict regimen that would allow him to heal. For weeks I took him on a lead, walking round and round the ring, round and round. Then I sat on his back, and we went round and round the ring, walking. We began a trot, and we went lightly. Alert wanted to be ridden harder, but I pulled him. I didn't want to work against him, but I had to. When we were finished for the day, I put my arms around his neck and lay softly. I led Alert back inside the stable, murmured soft sounds to him, and felt tenderly over his leg.

But it was too late for him. In the spring he pulled up lame again, throwing me. The pattern of his life had been established: injury, restriction, and reinjury. I would have waited forever for those times he could be ridden.

The next day my mother spoke to me. "I have something to tell you. Miss Reba has talked to us, and we agree. We're worried about you riding Alert. It's not safe. No one can predict when he'll reinjure himself—just that he will. And when he does, he could fall. He could fall on you at any time."

"He's never fallen on me!"

"Miss Reba knows of a family with a farm where he can be outside and get exercise without being ridden. There's a girl there who will help take care of him."

I appealed to Miss Reba. We talked in the riding ring.

"Why can't I ride him lightly?" I pleaded. "Isn't that what I've been doing?"

She spoke more softly than I had ever heard her. "You cannot ride him. You can only control him." She dropped her cigarette and snuffed it under her boot. She was working her hands, working them away at nothing. "Not having is part of having, M. I hope—"

I cut her off bitterly. "You're going to tell me I need some ingenuity. Well, now I'm like you. I won't ride." She had only her lessons to give me.

The next morning I walked into the stable and found Alert's stall empty, the brass plate removed from the door. I wondered if the girl would keep his name, the most lovely and perfect name, for whoever knew what it meant exactly?

They would not tell me where he had been taken. My mother said, "It's better this way." I would always wonder where he was, look for him in every pasture. From the highway I would see him shuffling down a hill toward me. He would be the one in a group of horses that stood apart, back from the road, waiting for my touch. I would always watch him as the sun went down and the light thinned. I would smell the warm grasses as the darkness solidified and the fireflies came up, until I could not see him any longer. But I would always feel him there, silent and black as thought.

Zipper

In tenth grade I flunked Home Economics. There were many fingers in the pie of my defeat, so to speak: fear of failure, mechanical inaptitude, stubborn resistance and rebellion, queasiness around needles, impatience, boredom, animus toward the teacher, alien hopes and dreams, foggy attention to instructions, love elsewhere, incompetent role models, and dislike of small household implements like sewing kits. But the concrete causes were two. In the fall semester I couldn't master cinnamon rolls. Mine weren't light and fluffy; they wouldn't rise. So heavy were they that some girls, bound for culinary glory and holding their edibles aloft, called mine cinnamon rocks. The other difficulty was my failure to complete the A-line dress we needed to sew in the spring. I suffered many trials in making it, all of them memorably wrapped up in the zipper.

The A-line! It sounds like some railroad, fabled in song by Duke Ellington or Leadbelly. But it was nothing more than a frumpy sleeveless dress with a scoop neck, close above the waist and flaring loose below, practical in design and unflattering. At least I've never seen anyone look good in one, not even the models in the sewing catalog the teacher circulated. The dress ended smack-dab in the middle of the kneecaps. "Not an inch above nor an inch below, but right in the middle, girls, that's what we want," Miss Needlebaum liked to say in her singsong way. She chose it as a new style, contemporary, up-to-date. Though old-fashioned in her own attire, tall and formidable, black glasses, hard curls in her graying hair, sensible black shoes, she could be accused by no one of falling behind the times. According to Miss Needlebaum, we were learning to cut and sew in the best modern way, installing a zipper, not such a new item in itself, but the first true advance in fasteners for clothing in centuries. The school itself was new, with bright linoleum and crisp white lighting. The sewing machines were new too, though beyond me with their switches, levers, pedals, and choices.

The task was quite simple—lay the zipper over the reinforced slit in the yellow fabric with daisies and guide one side and then the other under the needle of the sewing machine. Miss Needlebaum made it sound easy enough.

On the first try I sewed the zipper to a piece of fabric that somehow lay on the machine but was not part of the dress. When I had finished, the dress was nowhere in sight of the zipper. I didn't feel too bad. Some of the other girls were a bit nervous too, breathing in little puffs as they concentrated on the task. Others were doing fine. A girl named Jill was exquisitely talented, seated in front of her machine steady as a cat on a windowsill and focused on her prey. She was a maestro. Miss Needlebaum circled us, complimenting and suggesting. When she saw that I had sewn the zipper to the wrong material, she was perplexed. She told me to tear out the zipper and try again.

I made my second installation. It didn't go well. The zipper could now be said to be part of the garment, but no one could put the dress on and zip it up unless of remarkable anatomy. Miss Needlebaum was no longer circling because only a couple of us were still working on the zippers. I slumped to the front of the room and lay the dress down before her. She examined it and clucked. She displayed a nervous tic in her right eye that I had not seen before. "We shall have to start over again," she said, twitching.

I snipped the failed zipper out of the dress and contemplated my situation. What was wrong? *Why* couldn't I install the zipper? I was not clumsy with my hands, which could guide and groom Alert and slip softly over his smooth face. The zipper was, I admit, a long one, running down the dress from the neck to the small of my back. But all the other girls had by now sewn the identical zipper into the identical dress. I remembered the boys, who were building model boats in wood shop, boats to survive the squalls. I resolved to give it a third, heroic try.

For the life of me I couldn't install the zipper in the dress. The dress, like something willful, just wouldn't comply. It refused to be zippered. The stitches zigzagged and missed, bit the teeth, and wandered off into a field of flowers.

I had sewn the zipper twice, removed the zipper twice, and installed it for a third time. The A-line was supposed to be inspected. I carried the yellow dress up to Miss Needlebaum, knowing with metaphysical certainty that she was not going to like this zipper. All the other girls, who had moved on to the finishing touches, studied me.

This time, peering intently at the crimped and fraying fabric, Miss Needlebaum spoke out loud. "My, my, look here. See what she's done this time." She seemed to be addressing someone not present, perhaps a memorable peer in dressmaking. "Improper, improper. Tear it out and start all over again," she said firmly. Now she was decidedly talking to me.

I limped back to my machine, the A-line dragging behind me. "Turnpike," I muttered. "Sack." (I thought the dress should bear some name that gave a good sense of it.)

The other girls giggled, and one sneered, "Zipper lips!" Jill said nothing but looked pretty happy.

I startled everyone by yelling at her: "You're Jill the Zipper and you're going to marry Jack the Ripper!" The effect of this critique, though striking, was transitory. I didn't have my zipper in, and she did.

I sat at my machine, ruminating on the phrase "Zip it up!" I had heard it regularly since I was a little girl. Though I rarely spoke when spoken to, my first-grade teacher had been forced to tape my mouth shut because of my low murmurings.

Lately there had been a greater urgency to the phrase because of the alignment of my teeth, which was not what my mother thought it ought to be. I wandered to thoughts of my checkup the summer after Gwen's wedding. I had been embarrassed to hear that I had a dozen cavities. Even Uncle James was taken aback. But he hadn't made me feel more shamed than I already was.

"My, how evenly your cavities are distributed," he said mildly. "Very unusual."

I began to feel I was a technical phenomenon. He asked pointed questions about my oral hygiene, and I admitted that the toothbrush purchased months ago looked perfectly new.

My mother was concerned about a gap between my front teeth. She asked Uncle James what measures could be taken. "As you can see," she told him, "her mouth presents difficulties. I have advised her not to smile until we can have it fixed."

Uncle James glanced into my mouth, then dealt my mother a withering look. "My dear," he said to me, "the space between your teeth is too slight to treat. It isn't doing any harm, and if I might add, it is a real mark of distinction. Perhaps you got the gap from our side of the family. I have one too." He pointed to his own incisors. "In time, the space will undoubtedly lessen and the situation normalize."

In light of my troubles with the zipper, I wondered whether Uncle James was right. Would the gap decrease? I doubted I would ever be as proud of it as Uncle James was of his. I pictured the zipper slashing across my mouth where my own teeth had once been. My lips were fixed together, and I could produce only mournful sounds.

The bell to end class reined in my thoughts. I stuffed the dress in my bag and headed for the bus ride home, resigned to a fourth and, I knew, hopeless effort.

On the bus I got mad again and ranted and raved to the face in the window about how stupid Home Ec was and how I hated A-line dresses. "It's a stupid dress and a stupid class."

The girl in the window hated zippers. She knew that an improved sense of self and life did not depend upon learning to put a zipper in. Once the zipper is in, it has you, painfully catching your skin in its teeth.

My mother didn't know any more about sewing than I did; we were comrades in our inability to sew. Most strange, since sewing machines were more common in homes than televisions. How was it my mother slipped free of the sewing tree? How did she grow up without a needle in her hand? Sewing was what girls learned.

The girl in the window reminded me that my mother's mother didn't sew either. We were carrying on a tradition of sorts, the refusal-to-sew tradition—so occult few know of it. My sisters sewed even without a machine in the house. They learned from their paternal grandmother and at school in Home Economics classes like the one I was flunking. They installed any number of zippers on the first try.

When I got home, my mother asked, "Why the long face?" I told her of my troubles. This was the first she had heard of the A-line. I hadn't wanted to upset her. We sat in glum companionship for a while.

I was perplexed by this new sense of camaraderie. It wasn't what I felt about my mother when it came to cleanliness. And her fixation on posture! *Stand up straight and pull in your stomach.* It was like being brave when we went to Uncle James, not screeching when something bit down on you. She didn't recognize the futility of her efforts. And she bit down hard on me! "What am I going to do? I'm about to flunk Home Economics because of this zipper."

I pulled out the dress, and my mother examined it. She looked anxious, then sad. She shook her head and said it was too late. The material had frayed, disintegrating into a fringe of threads. There was no fabric left to attach the zipper to.

I now knew that something awful and humiliating was going to happen. I thought no longer about pumping the pedal that moved the needle. I thought that all over the world there would always be sewing machines and young girls learning to follow yellowed patterns. I would not be counted among them. While the other girls modeled their A-line dresses, I could wear my sack in penance or go naked.

I couldn't get out of the scene to come. But it wasn't going to happen immediately, and this was so much worse. Shame here and now is much better than shame on the way. The best I can say about the interval is that suffering is said to educate the heart. You think about escape, but there isn't any. I couldn't mail the dress to Miss Needlebaum, and I couldn't wait where I was. The whole wheel of the universe was turning to lift me toward the next session of Home Economics. I had to go to sleep, get up the next morning, take myself to school, sit through the day until the final period. There was nothing to be done but deliver my dress for the last judgment.

When the night had passed and the many hours of waiting, the moment came. I dropped the dress on Miss Needlebaum's desk and said, "I can't do it."

But now she surprised me. She was not in the least irritated; Miss Needlebaum looked pleased with me. I felt a quick moment of peace—until she sang, "Gather round and look, girls." They hurried up to the front of the room and bowed their heads over my yellow dress with the daisies. I stood frozen, eyes staring through the hole in the dress. Pointing to the place where the zipper should have been, Miss Needlebaum chanted, "What will become of her, what will become of her?"

All was quiet. No one moved or spoke. My tongue was thick. I could not answer the question. But then I felt anger in the bottom of my mouth. I could not see that the girls who managed the dress were the wiser for having done so. Quite the opposite. There were their faces around me. The dress with no zipper lay between us. On one side, Miss Needlebaum and the girls soon to be grown up true to her pattern—and I on the other, someone unknown.

I took one route and not another because of the zipper, there's no doubt about that. It set me going, or kept me going, in a particular direction, away from Jills and Needlebaums. I can hardly return now and say all that it meant. I couldn't sew the zipper; I couldn't control my hand. Still, as I think back, there's something sliding and changeable about zippers. A zipper goes up and down, it goes back and forth, it joins, it puts asunder, yes I will, no I won't. If the two sides part, like distrust or hatred or divorce, they also come back together again, like friendship or marriage or love. But everything depends on which side of the divide you're on. Sometimes it's good if there is no alignment, when the other side is Needlebaums or the captivity in Egypt.

Now, when the waters parted, I found myself on my mother's side.

Equestrians

In the driveway a station wagon waits for me. I am moving down the steps to get inside. The engine idles as if angry, and the doors tremble. The windows are closed mirrors, and in them the house behind me bends like a huge, nervous hand. I cannot see the driver. My fingers grip around the handle, and I depress the stiff button with my thumb. I lean away, step inside, and pull the door closed to hear it latch. I brace against the floor and feel the pressure of the seat beneath my legs and at my back. The vinyl is cracked, and there are crumbs of food and a smell both alive and dead. Outside, the doors say *Lillian Thurman School for Girls*.

The road passed through tall iron gates, skirted a swampy pond and horse corral, and came to an end in a circular drive that lay below a gothic building atop a short hill. A girl in uniform was standing at the curb. We exited the car, and she said, "Start with chapel. Through the main building and to your left." She pointed up the hill.

We climbed the steps and entered the gothic structure. Other girls in uniforms were hurrying through. We came out the back doors and saw to our left a modern one-story building of pink brick. Twenty or so girls stood in a line that started at a forbidding rosewood table set up beside the front doors. There were two women, one staunch and gray-haired, who stood in front of the table, and one small and white-haired, who sat behind it.

We got in line. We budged forward, and I saw that as each

girl reached the front, she made a curtsy and said, "Good morning, Miss Tanner." This seemed to acknowledge both women. Some of the girls took off an item of clothing or jewelry and laid it on the table. Then each knelt on a small square of rug, and Miss Tanner checked the length of her uniform. She pressed a ruler down against the front of the knee, as if installing wall-to-wall carpet, and measured the fabric that lay under the ruler.

When our turn came, Sally went first. Her skirt was a perfect two inches. I was next, and though I was a little too long, Miss Tanner said nothing and nodded for me to get up. When it was Harper's turn, Miss Tanner didn't need any ruler. She said dryly, "Your skirt is too short. The hem is to measure exactly two inches below the knee. Have your mother alter it." Miss Tanner held out her hand. "And scarves are not part of the uniform. Give it to me, please."

Miss Tanner had been headmistress at Lillian Thurman for thirty-five years. She lived with her mother in a house at the school and wore effective shoes because she walked briskly everywhere.

The driver is a man in his forties with a droopy mustache. I start to get in the back door. He says, "Hey, come on in front. Sit up here with me." I say nothing and get into the backseat. The driver grunts, rolls up his window, and shoots up the street. Then he rolls down his window, hollers "Heads up!" and spits out into the air.

Sally and I waited for Harper and then entered the chapel. The floors were highly polished wood without coverings. Rows of straightbacked chairs occupied most of the room. It doubled as an auditorium for dramatic productions, and the organ sat on the left side of the stage, which was hung with purple velvet curtains emblazoned LT.

One of the requirements for graduation from Lillian Thurman, a holdover from its early history, was completion of a needle-point seat cover, and these adorned the straightbacked chairs. No two covers were exactly alike. Some were colorful, some dull, some roughly done, one or two very beautiful in design and making. Lying on the seats were sheets of paper that listed the morning's hymns. We were among the last to sit down, and just then the chaplain came onstage, and we sang.

The chaplain gave a sermon, or rather he explained that he personally had been helped by prayer, and he made announcements about the business of the school. One of the boarders, a girl whose name I didn't catch, had climbed down the fire escape and run away during the night. The chaplain said that each of us was unique, like the covers on the chairs. He pointed out that there was more rejoicing in heaven over a lost sheep who had come back to the fold than over ninety-nine who had never strayed.

I leaned over to Harper and whispered, "I wonder why she ran away before school even started."

"Smart girl," she said. "Doesn't need school."

The chaplain led us in a prayer for the lost one.

The next rider is ready in front of her house. She is standing on the left side of the street, and the driver swerves over and stops with his window directly in front of her. He rolls it down. She has soft eyes and short blond hair, and her uniform is very neat. It is like a chambermaid's dress, pink with a white scooped collar and short puffed sleeves, plus a pink belt, white bobby socks, and saddle shoes.

She starts to reach for the rear door, but the driver says, "Hey, why don't you ride up here?" He pats the front seat and circles with his arm for her to walk around the front of the station wagon. She looks unsure. "Come on, honey. Sit up front with me. It's okay." He gives a little laugh to show it's okay. "Be a good girl, sit with me." I look at her and roll my eyes. She gets in back with me.

The English teacher, Mr. Himmelfarb, arrived in class a few minutes late. He was in his mid twenties and had a red beard. When he rolled up his sleeves, you could see the reddish blond hair move over the muscles in his forearms. He had a wide mouth, and his chin was hidden behind his beard. His plump lips seemed to move by themselves when he spoke.

The last girl lives in one of the row houses downtown. She comes out and strides down the walk when the driver honks the horn. It is hard to tell how old she is, though she must be my age. Her face is firm as a prow, a face you could see emerging out of fog in a deserted harbor. Her uniform is too short, but baggy, and she has flung an illegal scarf around her neck.

The driver asks her to ride in the front: "Keep me company, I'm lonely." She sees the two of us in the backseat and gets in the front door.

She turns to us and says, "Why are you both in the back?" We roll our eyes to indicate the driver. She shrugs her shoulders and says, "Well, my name is Harper, and yes it's an unusual name."

"I like unusual names," I say, but she doesn't seem to hear me. She is wrapping her scarf around her neck, around and around, for it is quite long.

At lunch, the dining room was murmuring with a hundred conversations. We were to use quiet voices inside at all times. Some of the teachers were sitting together at their own set of tables. Mr. Himmelfarb was there, laughing out loud and eating heartily.

I found Harper in one of the long rows of student tables. She was eating in the very way she walked—with the purpose of getting somewhere—while reading a book called *Rasselas*.

I set down my tray and said, "How can you eat this dreck?" In front of her were the same oily soup and dinner roll that looked almost grizzled with experience.

She smiled. "Whatever I have to eat just falls into my mouth."

I could think of no reply. She told me about herself. She had taken the subway to school in New York. Her parents were still young, though she was the oldest of several children.

I told her about my family and concluded, "I suppose you don't like your parents."

"No," she replied, "I love them, but they find me troublesome. I *am* rebellious. That's why they sent me here. They think Lillian Thurman will channel my energies. What about you?"

"I wasn't doing well in public school. My parents wanted me to go where I could learn higher things." I decided not to mention Home Ec.

"What kind of higher things?"

"Oh you know, Latin and stuff. My mother believes Latin is the root of all knowledge. I don't get it, but maybe I will after studying it." Saying it out loud sounded pretty silly, so I decided to try and chew my roll.

There were classes in Latin, French, history, and math. The best part of the day came at the end. It was a free period, and we could do what we wished. There were horses to ride. Harper was new to it, but I told her I would help her and that she would learn quickly. At Lillian Thurman riding was treated as a form of needlepoint; we could mount the horses from a two-hundred-year-old mounting block or be lifted into the saddle by stable boys. But we paid no attention. I began to teach Harper what Miss Reba was teaching me.

We soon fall into a routine in our trip to school. Sally and I sit in the rear seat, Harper in the front. The driver often stops to buy donuts.

"I used to buy my wife donuts," he tells Harper, "before she got fat. She used to be skinny like you, nice and skinny."

Harper says, "I'm not skinny."

"Her favorite were the cream filled. Now I won't buy her donuts. I'll buy *you* donuts instead."

"You should buy her donuts."

"No no, no more donuts."

We crawl along in the morning traffic. Then the way clears and the driver races ahead. Sometimes I say, "Look out!" to draw his attention back to the road, from which we seem continually to be slipping.

Again to Harper the driver says, "Eat, you're too skinny. You need some of these jellies in you," pointing to the box of donuts open on the seat. Harper pushes his hand away when it slips off the box onto her legs. All the way to school he promotes the donuts.

Among private girls' schools, Lillian Thurman ranked low. Girls came because they had not been accepted anywhere else or because their parents couldn't afford a better school. There were boarders and day students. Many had been packed off to board because they weren't wanted at home. They interfered with the free flow of their parents' lives, or they were too troubled to handle any longer at home. Parents said they were attracted to Lillian Thurman because it had been in existence for over two hundred years and they liked the school crest, but in truth they liked it because there were no boys, we wore uniforms without jewelry or makeup, the school was run by a single woman who had lived her whole life with her mother, and we attended chapel every day.

My mother withdrew me from my previous school because—besides Home Ec—I had taken to wearing bangles on both arms, stacked from the wrist to the elbow, and shaking them hard in response to any question I was asked. Miss Tanner demanded answers and did not neglect a girl's posture. My parents warned me that if I did not behave, I too could become a boarder.

Mr. Himmelfarb lived in one of the faculty houses, although the previous summer he had become engaged. Mr. Himmelfarb was too interested in our private affairs. "Have a hot date?" he'd ask Harper on Monday morning when she came into class looking disheveled.

One day he asked Sally how she had chipped her front tooth.

She looked embarrassed. "It was at camp last summer where I was a counselor. We were on a hike, and one of the campers was too tired to walk anymore so I was giving him a shoulder ride."

"You must have strong legs," said Mr. Him.

"But then I started to feel very strange and hot and all of a sudden I fainted. I hit my mouth on a rock." Him's lips made a little smile.

"The boy was okay though," Sally added anxiously.

Him was very interested in Sally's mouth and looked at it so much that she developed the nervous habit of covering it with her hand.

Sally and I usually squinch down low. The driver readjusts the rearview mirror to find her face or mine. He cranes around and asks us questions: "How many hours do you study? I used to be a teacher, you know." Sometimes he asks Sally about her grades, which are good. He says to me, "I hope you study more than Sally." If I study more than Sally, he tells Sally to study more. If I study less, he tells her that she can't be very bright. Sally sometimes cries. I learn to be silent. At stoplights he complains: "I can't believe I have to drive you scintillating conversationalists to school."

Sally develops an ulcer and loses fifteen pounds.

Harper's rebellion wasn't just what she did, it was what she failed to do. It began concretely. She stopped taking showers. "I'm in training for a wilderness retreat," she said. "Washing every day only makes us notice the dirt more. It's a question of perception."

She didn't wash her hair or have it cut and styled. She just let it grow out. The funny thing was, the more she gave in to not keeping herself up, the cleaner she appeared to be. Except for her hair.

People would look at its odd lengths and ask, "Are you growing it out?"

"Out from what? My head? Of course." She gave her hair a tug.

Him had us write stories. All my stories were about leaves falling off a lone Japanese maple. There were stories about a young girl who drives her car into the Japanese maple, causing the leaves to fall, and coincidentally killing her. There were stories about piles of leaves banked around the tree, the wind scattering the leaves, the rain plastering the leaves, children kicking the leaves, the moonlight making the leaves appear eerie, and a fox with a long tongue stealthily sleeping under the leaves. One story, in the form of a sermon, treated the vanquishing of the leaves of our lives. The style was very close to Martin Luther, whom I had been reading in history class.

Him, baffled by the obsessive quality of my writing, inquired whether there was some special significance to Japanese maples and falling leaves in my life.

I replied, "No, I have never seen one that I know of."

"Why don't you write about what you know," he suggested. "What do you know, what do you like to do?"

"I like riding horses."

"Horses?" He rolled his eyes.

He told me I had a cast of mind more critical than creative and to steer clear of trees in my writing.

Harper refused to wear underwear.

She wasn't motivated by a personal disgust or a desire to garner attention. She had traced the evolution of undergarments, didn't see a present need for them, and was opposed on principle. She said, "It simply isn't necessary, and I make it a point to avoid the unnecessary."

I don't know which outraged the other girls more—Harper's ability to pronounce her opinions or the absence of underwear. No one could get over the fact that under Harper's uniform was—her flesh. When the word reached a shocked Miss Tanner, she called Harper to her office.

I waited outside to hear what had happened. "What did she say?" I asked when Harper came out.

"She said, 'Harper, you must put your underwear back on.'"
"What did you say?"
"'Miss Tanner, I don't have any.'"

Him had us write poems of different sorts. One was supposed to be about a person we secretly admired. We were to read them aloud to the class.

When Harper's turn came, she looked at me and said, "Last night I wrote M's poem." I turned to stone.

> She is a rider of horses
> A rider to nowhere
> A lover of apples
> Whose juice they share.

The other girls were nodding. Him seemed to take it as a rebuttal.

I sit for hours at the Sears electric typewriter my father has bought me. I begin to get up in the middle of the night, agitated to write down dreams. When I wake in the morning, I rush the typewriter with a poem bursting in my brain. I can't stop the poems or the dreams from coming. I take up crocheting to calm my nerves. I sit on my bed facing the desk with the typewriter, crocheting a rug out of twine on an immense hook. In no time at all I leap up in a fit to type—what, I hardly know—and then, satiated, I return to my rug. The rug grows as large as my room.

My parents are disturbed by the noise of my typewriter in the middle of the night. I tell them I am a poet and that I am typing poems.

My father says, "Oh sure, you and my brother." My Uncle James is vaguely known to be artistic, to paint a little.

"Uncle James isn't a poet," I point out.

"No, he's a dentist, and that allows him to paint landscapes. What are *you* going to be?"

My mother reminds me of the poem she wrote with me in Miss Joy's class. We received a Dreadful. "How can you be a poet with that beginning? Why don't you just keep a diary?"

"Well, that was your poem, not mine."

They are perplexed. Who produced me, they wonder, looking accusingly at each other. It is an affront, really, calling myself a poet.

The argument swells, and there is yelling. My parents talk about family counseling but decide I am the one with the problem, not they. My father mentions the possibility of boarding.

I stop typing my poems. Only riding calms me now.

Him asked me to read my poem aloud in class. I opened my folder and got out "Afternoon Bath in the Sea," congratulating myself on the resemblance to a famous painting. The poem is not about leaves falling or horses but my new subject—diving off rock cliffs into a turbid sea and there being tossed and tumbled, pulled under until the breath is knocked out of me. I have written many poems on this subject, most involving my bathing suit being ripped off and other acts of violent exposure. It is my subject: fatalism.

When I finished reading the poem aloud, I looked around the room. The girls wouldn't meet my eyes.

Him began. My manner of reading was distasteful, but more to the point was the poem itself. He asked if the title was meant to be ironic.

Ironic?

"If so, it's a ghastly use of irony." The premise was implausible and overblown. My imagination had run away with me.

The image of a runaway train unfortunately pops into my head. I see Him on the side of the tracks trying to flag me down, to no avail. As I tear past, I wave and toot the horn.

My parents insist I go out with a boy from our church. It is part of an ongoing argument I am losing. I tell them I don't trust him, that he doesn't seem right in the head. He has an after-school job at a funeral home.

They say, "He goes to our church. He's okay."

I accompany him to his senior prom. It is a morbid affair. My corsage is plucked from a recent burial, and we travel in a hearse. We sit in a corner watching the other couples dance. No one talks to him. It turns out he is a junior, not a member of the graduating class.

I refuse to go out with him again. He shoots holes in our mailbox and garage doors. My parents blame me for the accident and make me pay for the repairs.

One Friday morning Harper told me that Sally was not going to ride the mad taxi anymore. She was going to board, moving right onto Lost Corridor, the most distant and dark wing of the second floor in the main dormitory. I could not digest it. What could she have done? Sally, a good girl, not wild, docile, nice, pretty. She did well in class. She never broke the rules.

I tracked her down at lunch. "Sally, what did you do?"

"I'm boarding," she said brightly. "I have the biggest and best room in the whole dorm."

"But what have you *done?*"

Her eyes were darting quick. "I haven't done anything." She started to put her hand to her mouth, then stopped. "I asked to."

It is spring, and I am out for a driving lesson with my father in his turquoise Cadillac. We're on a two-lane road, and suddenly I am stuck behind a parked postal truck. The driver is off on foot to deliver a package. Cars stack up behind me. My father grows exasperated and says, "Go around, for godsakes, go around." The cars are angry idling behind me, and my father's face is getting red. I crank the wheel counterclockwise, press on the gas a little, and try to go around. We clip the rear panel of the truck, and then we're lodged against it. I jam down the accelerator to get moving. The rear bumper is pried away from the Cadillac, and off we go.

As her farewell to the school year, Harper was caught smoking. She was suspended for the last week of class. I was baffled because Harper didn't smoke.

I told her, "I am angry that you have gotten yourself suspended for an offense that has no meaning."

"Don't worry," Harper smiled. "I'll write to you."

We are having dinner. I mention that I will soon have my driver's license. There will be no need for transportation to Lillian Thurman in the fall.

I have complained about the driver before. "It's stupid for me to be driven to school by that moron."

"We're not much concerned with his intellect," my father replies. "He's supposed to get you to school, no more."

"He's a maniac! He's dangerous!"

"What do you mean?" my mother joins in. "I haven't heard that he's been in any accidents." That is, with postal trucks.

My father nods. "Your own recklessness has put an end to any possibility of your driving to school."

I am outraged by the injustice of it all. "I'm not going to ride with that filthy man anymore! If that's the only way to get to school, I won't go!"

The muscles in my father's jaw are bulging. Then they smooth down, and he says with a little smile, "Fine. You won't ride with him? Don't ride with him. You can be a boarder."

Harper also became a boarder in the fall.

"What happened? You didn't write to me."

"I ran away over the summer," she explained. "I came home bruised one day, ran off again, and married a musical prodigy. Now he's off being a priest. He told me I was a fool to believe in destiny and that I'd marry again. My parents had it annulled."

I crimped my lips to show what I thought of this story.

"Okay, he was a boy working on his doctorate in Chinese. A

sculptor named Marco Polo who liked to spray paint his art. It was not against my parents. It's nothing personal."

Harper's rebellion was abstract; her parents just happened to get in its way. My rebellion was personal; my sense of resistance began inside and worked its way outward. I was painfully aware of my anger and wore it like a hand-me-down because as yet I had nothing with which to replace it.

"What about you? Why are you here?"

"Oh, I ran into a postal truck, Alert is gone, and I don't want to live at home ever again, not exactly in that order."

Harper and I were assigned rooms on the Lost Corridor. We were at the back of the building with the fire escapes. My room was side by side with Sally's. I could sometimes hear her moving about, or sometimes crying.

Harper turned her room into an ashram. Incense burned. You had to take your shoes off when you entered. She stopped eating meat and talked about the purifying effects of liquids. She drank herbal tea out of weighty mugs. She read the Bible on Sundays, the only scholar I knew among the students.

The senior class decided that for the yearbook each girl would choose a spot in which to be photographed and a quotation to represent her. The day our class photos were taken was a warm, early October day—the roses were still blooming, the trees still in leaf. Many of us had chosen spots away from the school buildings, in a part of the campus where the oldest trees stood. I climbed one of the largest, given my fondness for trees. You could see initials carved in neat rows on the trunk facing the camera.

One night I woke up to hear a thumping on the wall, coming from Sally's room. I listened for a minute, then went to Sally's room, but it was locked. The thumping kept up. I woke the housemother, who had a key.

Sally was beside her bed in her nightgown, kneeling with her face against the wall, as if she were praying or having her skirt measured. She was sobbing through her hands and banging her forehead against the wall, even and slow as a minuet.

She had taken two months' worth of birth control pills. That night she was whisked away to a private hospital. Her mother came to pack up her belongings while we were in class.

A dream: little children have come to Harper and me for riding lessons. We have ten strong horses, fat on winter grass. Harper and I teach them the voice that horses listen to, the touch that horses feel. We show them the warm pressure of thighs, how their muscles will move the horses forward. Even so, there is no preparation that prepares. In the spring, the children and horses make a swim across the swamp. The horses move slowly out of the corral, down the long lane. They shy away from the swamp, for dry land, scrub brush. The children urge their horses into the water. One is Sally. She forgets the warm pressure of thighs and whispers. The horses plow through long weeds and water, turning fish out of season. She grips too hard. Her horse loses her footing, her mane and tail a remembrance. The swamp is thick with horses, their riders hanging onto the reins. Harper carries the drowned girl across the neck of her mount to shore. The survivors take their horses into the woods.

Harper said, "She played the role of the conventional girl, the good daughter, the ordinary sister. She was impressed by his sophistication, which would be spotty and hollow to someone more experienced. She was an object against which he could play out his vanity. I tried to listen, but I never heard him."

Two days later, Mr. Himmelfarb quit Lillian Thurman. We watched him climb into his MG. On his way out he stopped in front of us and spat out at Harper: "You have your head screwed on crooked and you're going to be real trouble for someone."

There were changes when Sally left. Harper moved into the large room next to mine, where Sally had been. And Mr. Idleheart came to replace Him. He had three grown daughters and had been at a prestigious girls school for many years before descending to Lillian Thurman.

I wondered why a man of his stature would come to our school. He looked distinguished. He dressed very well and wore expensive shoes and drove a big Lincoln. He had nice manners and listened politely when you spoke to him.

"He's a lot better than Him, isn't he?" I said to Harper.

"He melts in your mouth," she answered.

Harper and I kept to our rooms on Lost Corridor. We never rode. We recited poetry to each other to the rhythm of a tom-tom. From the hall we heard, "What are you doing in there? Are you beating drums?" Her shoes out in the hall, cross-legged in the middle of the candlelit, incense-filled room after lights out, Harper read to me from *Soul on Ice*. On Sundays we listened to Nina Simone and Otis Redding. We listened hard, trying to understand.

We had been given up on by nearly everyone, and we were trying to create ourselves out of paltry materials in a hostile place. We had nearly given up on ourselves.

Harper was changed. She was quiet, she watched TV, she stopped reading, she shaved her head. She was intent on flunking her courses. She devoted herself to doing nothing.

Where had her boldness gone? It was a botched job, a messy business, rebelling. Hard to sustain.

"What are you hanging around me for?" Harper said. "I have no time for you, girl. 'If thou hast done foolishly in lifting up thyself, or if thou hast thought evil, lay thine hand upon thy mouth.' A pimp found me, and I became a whore. A rebellion against rebellion."

I decided to talk to Mr. Idleheart about my concerns. "I'm

worried about Harper," I told him one day after class. I speculated that it might be drugs. If so, I assured him, it was still in
the early stages. "But I'm afraid something terrible is going to
happen. Please don't tell Miss Tanner, because she would certainly tell Harper's parents, and that would be the worst outcome."

Mr. I promised he would talk to Harper and say nothing to
Miss Tanner.

One night I heard a thumping against the wall. I listened for a
minute. I knew what it was. It was the banging of the bed in
Harper's room. I got up and looked out at the fire escape. A pair
of excellent shoes was sitting outside her window.

When it was over, I got back in bed and thought about Him
and Mr. Idleheart. Why not Him? Getting involved would have
been giving in. It was a rebellion against her own freedom. But
what was this? I thought about apples, when the last one would
drop.

The next morning I thought I'd shock her, and I spoke bitter
words when we met. "What's with the shoes? Is that so no one
can hear him climb the fire escape?"

"No," she said, looking straight at me. "You know you have
to take off your shoes when you come in my room."

That's the way I find her; we make our tea and read our books
and then the English teacher makes love to her. The pin in your
head snaps. I am in my room when I hear your head fall. You
are rolling laughing. Stop Stop that knock in your head—you
laugh my name.

Harper was gone before the end of the term. The needlepoint
seat was waived, and I graduated. I wore a long white gown and
carried a red rose, as if in rehearsal for marriage. My name was
called and I slowly walked to Mr. Idleheart. He handed me a
diploma and gave me a congratulatory kiss.

I still believe that people are really good at heart. Knowledge is not wisdom. I will study and get ready, and perhaps my chance will come. Put your troubles into the bottom of your trunk, then sit on the lid and smile. Under the photograph of Mr. Idleheart, Shakespeare's words—*He was a scholar, and a ripe and good one; exceedingly wise, fair-spoken, and persuading.* I'm looking down at the photographer, and in the light coming through the leaves in black and white I seem to blend into the branches, as if I were floating. My words are *Leaves, leaves, turn and tell me what I am.*

Harper is seated on the ground. Her head, neck, and upper body fill the photo. I can just make out a fringe of trees in the background. Her hair is loose, blown back off her face. She looks with certainty at the camera and beyond.

> Sometimes I feel I have to
> express myself
> and then, whatever it is I have
> to express
> falls out of my mouth like flakes
> of ash . . .
> (I ask) to be special, and alive
> in the mornings if they are
> green . . .

I know the words beneath her by heart. There is no end to surviving, the voice, the touch, the warm pressure moving forward, and the gripping too hard.

Tomatoes

There was a woman I knew in college not because I wanted to. I called her the tomato woman because that's what she was, a woman in love with tomatoes, and because of her, I touched tomatoes again, though I had sworn in sixth grade, after Miss Joy, that I wouldn't.

Through the tomato woman I found out that there were more rules, not just about what and how to eat, but about what it meant to be a woman, about fertility, about the color red, and about small round spheres. The tomato woman considered *me* a woman, though I was confused by the question of when I would officially become a woman. There seemed to be any number of stops along the way to choose from.

She was the wife of a professor whose course on World Hunger I was taking. He was also my adviser, and his first act as such was to enroll me in his course. We were flirting, the professor and I, on the outskirts of having an affair. It would be my first. Up till then my experience had been with what you'd have to call boys, even if they were themselves in college. I knew nothing about the perils of flirting with a married man.

After one of his classes on crop rotation, he said with some bitterness, "I can't work at home, there are so many children. No house is big enough to hold us. My wife is always in the garden or making meals, providing, providing, providing, but it's making me fat."

We were leaning in the hall outside his office. I thought to say he should stop having children or buy a bigger house, but before I could form the words he said, "You opened a way to the place I keep hungry. My wife has chained me to a refrigerator."

I was about to say that I didn't see any refrigerator, and then thought better of it. I supposed he was talking metaphorically and that this was what romance was.

I said, "I stay away from edibles." With that, he ushered me into his office, closed the door, and kissed me on my thin, colorless lips.

As the semester progressed and her husband spent more and more time at his office, the professor's wife took an interest in me. She sensed a rival, as women are wont to do. One day she arrived unexpectedly on campus after a class on the merits of alfalfa, a crop my professor thought much underrated. I remembered that it had grown near the house on Twenty-second Street and thought it unexceptional.

She favored red, witness her mouth scarred with vermillion lipstick. She asked me to drive home with her, to eat fresh tomatoes from her splendid garden. Her plants were still producing, she told me proudly, though it was late October. She told me that every woman loves a tomato: "It's red, it's round, it's nutritious—it's life, for godsakes," she chanted, as if speaking to the foolish female multitudes. It was then I noticed her car was indeed red, fire engine red.

I said, "I hate the way sliced tomatoes lay inert on cold white plates. Lizzie Borden hated tomatoes. She was a woman, wasn't she?"

But in her enthusiasm she didn't notice. She said, "Life is probably round, like a tomato, don't you think?"

I was pale, thin, wore black, and smoked. I was unhealthy. My hair smelled of smoke and bars. I crossed my legs and never trusted.

I told her, "With tomatoes, I get sick; in fact, because of an unfortunate early experience I might tell you about, I get sick at the very idea of milk or tomatoes. Mixed together, they are poison. You see, I only drink gin, eat peanuts, and smoke cigarettes. That's my daily fare. When I put homemade bread or wheat germ or garden-grown vegetables, especially tomatoes, into my body, I'm not well. My body won't tolerate them. It spits them out."

She was aghast. She was about to swerve off the road, and I grabbed the steering wheel to keep us from wrecking then and there. Having righted herself, she repeated what had already become too familiar: "Every woman loves a tomato. You will too, eventually."

Entering the house, mulling over the word *eventually*, I thought, I guess I'm not a woman then, because I won't ever love tomatoes, of that I am sure. Tomatoes, red, round, and plump, lined up on a sunny windowsill, remind me of the joyless conformity of sixth grade, of tomato aspic, of women dead in their thirties.

She was going to fix me a tomato shake she was certain would change my life. "You can join me in the kitchen, if you like," she said.

"Not in this life," I said under my breath. While she ground away in the kitchen, I wandered through the house, counting the cribs—six of them. I imagined each baby had an extravagantly red cherry tomato, perfectly symmetrical, stuck in its mouth, and with each breath, the tomato was sucked in and out, in and out, silently.

Within minutes, the World Hunger professor arrived home for a lunch of roasted pumpkin seeds and tomatoes. He was right on time; the clock had just struck noon. I wondered where his chain was. Chagrined to find me with his wife, he looked from her to me and back again, between bites. His wife handed me a tall glass of thick tomato foam. "This will give you color, dear, make men want to know you and touch you."

I said, with some heat, "You know, some things can't be changed. All my life all I've ever heard is to eat tomatoes. But I ask you, why should I if I don't like them."

"I didn't know you hated tomatoes," the husband uttered with a look that said, *My feelings for you have completely changed.* 133

He took up a tomato near him and, after turning it in his fingers for a long time, sank into the most profound contentedness.

I drank the entire concoction.

And then it happened—a terrible case of the hiccups. I put my head in a bag the tomato woman provided and bent my head down between my knees. Inside the bag, it was dark and wet with heavy leaves. I could see the breathing tomatoes of the tomato woman close to me; they were brushing up against my skin, in love with the touch of my pale skin. I thought, these are tomatoes, then, the great round world of tomatoes that has been so anxiously and so often offered and refused, and I have touched them again, I have taken them inside me, I have drunk them. I drank them because the tomato woman dared me, because she thinks that I am in danger of losing myself, that the tomatoes will either change me or kill me, what amounts to the same thing. But she is just another Miss Joy with rules, rules, rules, and I will be the exception. The tomato woman and the World Hunger expert will have to face facts—every woman does not love tomatoes. Whether the justices declared the tomato a vegetable or a fruit in 1893 is nothing to me. Fresh or canned, as juice, puree, paste, ketchup, or chili sauce, the tomato is not an inspiration for culinary uplift. I don't care if they're creamed, puffed, stuffed, canned, Creole, custard, green, grilled, preserved, scalloped, or stewed, I hate tomatoes. Dress them up, dress them down, disguise them, mask them, douse them with lemon, sit them next to a shrimp, a tomato is a tomato: I don't believe in transcendence.

The tomato woman and the professor, curious and concerned, had moved dangerously near. They were speaking the way couples speak who have been together a long time. I couldn't understand them. I dropped the bag from my face, and I vomited. On the top portion of the husband's shoes, where the tongue and laces meet.

"Some things are indigestible," I said as I stumbled for the door.

Jump

COURSE

I was enrolled in his writing course—Creative Writing, Phase 1— and knew he was married. After my affair with the World Hunger expert in my freshman year, I had sworn off such forays. The problem was I found dating men my own age like riding lesson horses: they were too tame and predictable. They were for beginner riders, which I no longer considered myself to be. You couldn't go very fast on them, and yet they made more of the date than it deserved. An older man, I thought, would be less inclined to solidify.

BATTLE OF THE SEXES

English 271, meanwhile, met across the hall from his office. I had been assigned an oral report on George Eliot's *Adam Bede* and had stayed up all weekend preparing for Monday afternoon's seminar. When I arrived, half the students were missing. The other half hadn't finished reading the book. Class was canceled, and I stomped out, steamed that I wasn't going to give my report. As I paused outside, too furious to turn this way or that, he called my name. I turned around.

"Come in," he said. "Sit down."

COURSE

I was wrong. I was a rank beginner. I was adept at attracting men, the wrong men, but knew nothing about the stages after.

I was trying to move slowly to the ring and stay a cool distance from him.

BATTLE OF THE SEXES

"I understand why you are angry." He was agitated and moved into the imperative. "Now squeeze my hand."

SNOW

There are twenty-eight words in Eskimo for snow, and at least as many ways that he upset my family. He was married, for starters. Everything my mother had said about horses applied to him, and it all had the same effect: it made me want to ride him.

BATTLE OF THE SEXES

I shook my head. I didn't want to squeeze his hand.

"Go ahead, squeeze hard." He rested his elbow on his desk and wiggled his fingers as if he were limbering up to arm wrestle. I grabbed his hand and squeezed.

"Come on, harder."

He was squeezing my hand so hard I could barely breathe, and he looked just as hard into my eyes, which I wanted to close. He said, "If your eyes are brown or green, they're all the same to me. Now warm yourself over this fire." The room seemed unutterably hot.

"You need to open that window," I said, pulling my hand away.

SNOW

His father had shortened the family name when they arrived from Poland. They lived in Los Angeles, and thus my parents supposed they must be philistines. Los Angeles didn't have winter. The country club my parents belonged to did not admit their kind. *What kind of person could be produced in such heat?*

Touching him, I dropped a bomb on the village of my past. He had a history larger than mine.

COURSE

He introduced me to orgasms and Chinese food, artichokes and roasted boar, Godard, Buñuel, Bergman, and contempt. In that order.

SNOW

Whether it was a cuisine he favored or a style of dress or the way he spoke, he threatened everything my family had trained me to represent. Hence the attraction.

COURSE

He was a gambler and immoderate in the handling of all things. Sometimes he was flush, other times he didn't have a dime. Much had passed through his hands, including his wife. He never finished the food on his plate to prove he would never be as hungry as he had once been.

SNOW

My family's code: Hide your unhappiness. But he attended pool marathons at his mother's house where her patients experienced rebirth, passing one another down a birth canal made of hands. He had been reborn many times.

BATTLE OF THE SEXES

Did he do this kind of thing regularly? He opened the window, which looked out on a ravine. By the window hung a photograph of a woman, his wife.

COURSE

The affair should have expelled me forever from the familial garden. But the plan went awry. I didn't have the nerve. I was like a rider approaching a very solidly constructed jump, a triple rail, and instead of leaning into the jump at the necessary moment, becoming one with my horse, I pulled back, a hesitation my horse read like radar.

BATTLE OF THE SEXES

She stared down from her position on the wall at our strange blood grip.

COURSE

My horse pulled up—balked at the start of the jump, when rider and horse should be lifting together if they are to have any chance of clearing the rails. My horse cut away, and I sailed through the jump, mountless.

SNOW

Choosing him would be the last straw, the final disappointment, the act of rebellion that could not be forgiven.

COURSE

Nothing happened as I imagined. I took the jump, but I bungled it badly. Like my mother swimming. You can't look back, you have to look straight ahead, focusing on the jump. When you jump, you think *clear.*

SNOW

My family was shocked; however, they did not expel me from their ranks, as I had predicted. They pulled in tighter, determined that if anyone was going to cut ties, it was going to be me.

COURSE

Since birth, I had failed many times in my attempts at self-creation.

BATTLE OF THE SEXES

Few words were said, and most of those were his.

COURSE

If he had been able to give me a transfusion everyday, I might have cleared the jumps. He couldn't spend his life squeezing my hand and looking hard at me.

SNOW

They gambled I couldn't. I was still attached, by the frailest thread, to the mother who had crossed out the space where my pictures were to be in the baby book.

They were right. I couldn't give as good as I was getting.

Recipes

While I lay in my professor's bed, languishing, I thought about my distaste for order and about the mess I was making of my life. Lying in my married professor's bed was not where I was supposed to be. And he was not whom I was supposed to be with. The concept of order, that is, assigning places where things belong and assuming the stages of my life as they were set out for me, never took. I heard the word—*order*—but it didn't sink in. I never knew where anything belonged. Was this because I didn't know where *I* belonged or whom *I* might belong with? Nothing belonged to me. Not this bed, not this house. It was not where I was supposed to be.

I don't know exactly what I expected—heartbreak, I suppose, mostly mine. The affair would end when he too realized that he loved his wife. I was a fling. That's how I thought of myself—*the fling,* suitable for flinging. I was too young, too unready. There would be others more right for me. There would be scenes of parting, tearful speeches in barren wintry landscapes, and then life would go on, because it could. I imagined what he might say to end it. I agreed with every word.

But he never said those things, obviously true, that I was waiting for him to say. He said he was leaving his wife and wanted to marry me. He filed for divorce. We got engaged and rented a dark house with a gloomy kitchen. I quit school and rode the bus to a job answering the phone at a housecleaning service.

I tried to organize my new life by making lists of things to do. I was always losing things, misplacing them. Sometimes I made a list only to lose it minutes later. My lists were a mixture of the profound and the mundane, the ordinary and the mad, items I could check off and items that would never be checked off—that would repeat themselves forever.

I still have a list from this time. Soon after my engagement, Uncle James died suddenly from a heart attack, and I made the list on my flight home for the funeral. It shows that I had no priorities, the foundation of higher civilization, and no sense of what could be accomplished on a plane. You can read it from top to bottom or bottom to top; it makes no difference.

Throw out papers. [I refused to keep anything.]
Quit. [Quit what? Smoking? My job? Biting my nails?]
Straighten out Bank Accounts. [Capitalized]
Put screens in windows. Laugh more. [While putting in screens?]
Organize poems. [An item that appeared on all lists.]
Buy donuts.
Be successful.
Buy toothpaste and have a more positive attitude.
Lose ten pounds. [On every list. The number of pounds varies. If happy, it's five pounds. When drastic measures are required, it's twenty. The list never said, "Stay where you are, you're just fine."]
Change life. [Often, in some variation]

Toothpaste is on an equal footing with charting new behavior, changes I might work at for my whole life, with little success. Suppose I died, like Uncle James, suppose the plane crashed and those who mourned my passing interpreted this list as my last will and testament. How would they rank these items, order them? What might they say I had left undone?

No mention of the impending wedding.

To celebrate the engagement, my mother threw an informal party the day of my arrival home, a somber affair under the circumstances, inviting many of her oldest friends. It was a luncheon, with tomato-salmon aspic in the mold of a rolling pin. I couldn't eat a thing; it just jiggled on my plate between my knees.

The party turned into a sort of kitchen shower. I found this most strange, given my history. I received a hardbound copy of *The Joy of Cooking,* surely a gesture in jest. Were there cookbooks for those who approach the stove only under duress? What would such a book be called—*The Resistant Cook?* I sat and read: "The principles of cooking are to make no substitutions, take no liberties with the stated amounts, measure precisely, follow the steps in the order given, use the utensils specified and the pans, and, by all means, employ a timer; the right result is guaranteed to follow." In sum, the obedient would be rewarded. It sounded plausible enough, until I went on to the elaborate instructions "About Meat," which I didn't want to eat. These were prefaced by the following remark—"You will approach the butcher's counter in a nervous state because cuts look bafflingly similar." I decided not to approach the meat counter in any state. The instructions covered choice, grades, and degrees; did these terms refer to the animals' education? Low-quality young animals and meat from old animals was an eye-opener, since I had never considered age a factor. Storing, seasoning, mincing, grinding, pounding, macerating, moist-heat versus dry-heat methods, and my favorite—degrees of gray in browning. It reminded me of an off-Broadway play.

I used my list as a bookmark, and that's why I have it to this day.

The women had put together a little box—I couldn't help it, I kept thinking of a coffin—filled with what they called "recipes for a successful marriage." On the front was inscribed, "A recipe lovingly followed is an evocation of domestic harmony and an homage to marriage." When I flipped through I saw that they were written in a language I couldn't understand. I couldn't fathom the distinction between *crush* and *mince, chop* and *dice, sliver* and *grate, shred* and *peel.* One recipe, Chuck Roast in Foil, was targeted for informal company. It carried the tip "Do not cut the foil until you are at table and ready to serve. The sudden burst of fragrance adds to the anticipation." I couldn't understand why informal company should be treated to the burst of fragrance but formal company should not. Flank Steak Mixup—which had to be a mistake—suggested my own notion of hunger as a messy, tangled business. By Cake That Never Fails I was directed to add yellow food color, if desired. I had no such desires. I was told to add spices to taste, but I didn't know what they were supposed to taste like. There were cryptic commands like *Correct seasoning* and *Do not underbeat.* I realized that to be a good cook, you have to be clairvoyant. I doubted I'd ever have the knack, the coordination of hand and heart, for cooking. My heart was somewhere else. I did not want to stand facing the stove; if I were to stand anywhere, I would face a window.

Though she had never spoken in praise of the practical, my mother contributed a few recipes, scrawled in her indecipherable hand and different from the rest. They did not describe how to proceed; they lacked logical steps and instructions in technique. Ingredients were listed in no particular order, and amounts were vague. Reminders to herself, unconnected to the dish, about a bill to pay or a travel tip, were scribbled in the corners. I saw that if in a risky moment I decided to work from the recipes, I would have to invent a dish, like playing anagrams. I could never predict the result, though I was sure to be led into some culinary disasters. But I might also make something delectable, in a new mold, on an incline that had never been seen before.

The next day was Uncle James's funeral.

Uncle

It was small solace that I had not become engaged while Uncle James lived. It would have broken his heart to see his last niece walk down the aisle.

Neighbors had found him in the basement, stretched out on his back beside the washer and dryer, dead two days. At the reception, holding a glass of punch, Gwen murmured, "He was doing the laundry. He died instantly. He didn't feel a thing." His quick departure was supposed to make up for the two days he lay unremembered. No one mentioned that he lay on the basement floor, his long legs getting stiff, the dryer starting up every few minutes, the drum turning to prevent wrinkles, round and round.

I thought of my grandmother, who had died just a few months before Uncle James. By the time I was a child, arthritis had caught hold in her and flared through her body, crippling her. She could not take a real bath. Someone had to bathe her, the thick support stockings rolled about her thick ankles, her feet too swollen for shoes, the long underwear that never came completely off. Someone had to sponge her back, dipping the cloth into the sink. Someone had to wash her hair. She loved for me to take a bath on my Saturday nights there so she could hear the sound of the tap running and think of easing into the long bath. All her baths would be bubble baths, she said, with her body hidden under suds.

What was he washing? He wore a meticulous smock for dentistry. The load was probably a light one, for he lived alone since my grandmother had died a few months earlier. He, of course, would sort. Did he have shirts in the load? Was it underwear and socks, or towels, or sheets? Were his socks worn through at the heel, like mine? And who pulled the clothes from the wash? Bachelor uncles die alone, doing the laundry, and someone sifts in amazement through the last shriveled things. Who sifted through Uncle James's last load?

I was not my uncle, who managed to reach zero hour out of matrimony. I had inherited his aversion to wives, like the gap in his front teeth, but now that I was becoming one myself, the aversion turned to a severe complication. It appeared I had not inherited his ingenuity. I had not maintained my location outside matrimony. My life was a mix-up of allegiances, each bleeding its colors into the others, all under one roof. I could never keep things in separate piles. I could no longer identify what parts of my life belonged to love, even self-love, and what parts belonged to marriage. How could I extricate myself from one without losing the others? Uncle James put love to one side, marriage to the other. There had been no marriage, or a fleeting one, but had there been love for Uncle James? Of that I was uncertain.

He had warned me. "In marriage, one or the other has the upper hand. Either way, it's not pleasant." He thought my mother had the upper hand. When his brother married, he vanished. Had Uncle James known my mother before her transformation into his brother's wife, he might have mourned her as he mourned his brother. But he hadn't known her. When they first met, she was already engaged, and the disappearing act was under way. As for me, I was a small blur on the horizon, fading fast. I had already become this new and other entity called a fiancée, which took on a not-so-charming life of its own. How had it happened? To the best of my recollection, I had neither assented nor refused. I was a greenhorn rider, frozen at the jump. I had fallen on it, slipped on a patch of ice. And this time it didn't look as if anyone would save me.

He had a particular distaste for wives in fur coats, I recalled as I looked over the table of punch and crackers at the reception. But to my thinking wives with diamonds were worse, for they wore the symbol. I looked at Gwen's hand. She liked to flash her ring to suggest the magnitude of her husband's love. I saw the virtue of my mother's respect for a thin gold band. Why should a diamond be the sign of the wife? Why a stone? Durability? Expense? The diamond is such a cold stone, heartless. When women become wives, do they become colorless and cold and edgy? Nothing more depressing than a woman's hand, manicured, nails painted, fingers laden with the diamonds of marriage. Gwen's hands could not move, could not wave, could not brush the stray hair from her face, they were so weighted by love. I remembered Uncle James's words at her wedding: "The married couple can't cut away. Their marriage dawdles on and on, without the energy to die."

I looked down at my own hand and saw the small emerald. It wasn't a diamond, but what exactly was the difference? It didn't feel right on my hand. When I caught sight of it clearing a plate from the table, I wondered whose it was. It didn't belong to me; it wasn't attached to my arm, my body. I'd never been able to hold onto a ring before; the more studded with significance, the faster I'd lose it. My high school pinky ring didn't last a month before it was pulled off with a glove. I didn't feel its absence until hours later, when I noticed my naked finger. Another ring disappeared in a pool. No matter how many sweeps of the bottom I made, lingering over the drains where the pennies lay, I never found it. How did it just disappear?

Two days after the funeral we went through the house to disburse Uncle James's belongings. The downstairs was just as my grandmother kept it, old-fashioned, stuffy, dark chairs with ornate legs and embroidered cushions. But the upstairs was a surprise—no one had been aware of the extent of Uncle James's painting. The rooms were crammed with paintings, hung on every stretch of wall and stacked in the attic. Most of the subjects were familiar, the house at the shore, local winter landscapes, studies of the light inside the kitchen.

My father donated the bulk to a local art school, the family having picked two or three each to keep. I chose a painting that departed from the rest. It presented a surreal forest scene in earthy oils, brown, green, black, and chalky white. There were no bright hues. At the bottom of the frame were exposed roots of teeth, which turned into gnarled trunks as they rose, columns of dark color that stretched to the top of the frame and beyond. Firmly planted among the sinewy trees, a little to the left of center, was a man wearing an immaculate white garment like a toga, hanging loosely from one shoulder and falling across his body in drapes down to his feet. His arms and legs were dark and muscled, matching the trunks in color and torque. The imposing forest might have dwarfed him, but he was lifted forward, as if pulling himself into another plane.

Baby

A month before the wedding, I was on my way to work when a woman in her early thirties, wearing black biker's shorts and carrying a shoulder bag, stepped onto the bus and took a seat across from me. The warmth of her body moving down the aisle is still distinct. She braced her left hand against a rail and threw her bag across her lap. Then she stared at my engagement ring, which made me uncomfortable. I didn't feel sure of myself anywhere, even on a bus full of strangers. I had been twisting the ring about my finger.

The woman was looking from my ring to my face and back again as if trying to calculate a difficult sum. Then, sighing at the impossibility, she leaned toward me and asked, "Is that an engagement ring?"

I nodded.

"Emerald is an unusual choice, isn't it?"

I nodded again. I didn't want to encourage her. As it turned out, she wasn't easily discouraged.

She said, "I was young when I got married, too. Though I don't think I looked as young as you."

When salespeople came to the door, they asked if my mother was home.

"No one made me get married, I mean I didn't *have* to get married, if you get my drift." She wore stacks of rings on her fingers, but her wedding finger was bare. "I was young, too young. I hardly knew my left hand from my right, yes from no. It never occurred to me I could be a wife, much less a mother.

I moved directly from my parents' house to my husband's, with no stops in between. And then before you knew it, we had a baby."

Life was too short for this story.

She shifted her bag on her lap. "I wanted him, I mean, my husband and I decided after a lot of back and forthing, to do it, to go ahead, to just produce him, to deliver him into this world for all it was worth, which isn't, as you know, much. At any rate, we did the job, the seed was planted, and the baby was growing."

A moment's pause, then she went on. "You know, I didn't like it. I thought I would like it. But I didn't, I didn't like it at all. But I couldn't say that because I was supposed to love it. Absolutely *love* it. I was supposed to have been born to do this, make babies. You know, you grow up, get married, have a baby, that's the plot."

She looked out the window for a minute, then went on. "Nine gigantic months stretched out ahead of me. I'll tell you what was gigantic. The arguments I had with my husband were gigantic, the amount of food I ate was gigantic, my underpants were gigantic. My dresses looked like those drapes women wear in the South Pacific who sing lullabies from the rim of volcanoes. I asked myself, what was I growing, a couple of inches of flesh or a spaceship? I walked around the apartment in my bathrobe with my pockets full of potato chips. I had this feeling that someone or something was controlling my body. I asked the doctor about it. You know what he said?"

She looked at me but didn't wait for an answer. "He said, 'It's perfectly natural. All women feel this way. After all, you have someone living inside you—a close neighbor, so to speak.' But I ask you, what's natural about someone taking up residence in your uterus and then quadrupling in a couple of weeks?

"'You could cut down on your intake,' the doctor told me.

"I said, 'His or mine? If it was just me, I could slow down a bit. But what about him?'

"'What can I tell you,' he said.

"'Yeah, what can you say?'

"The final months were just awful, like everyone tells you after the birth, not before. I couldn't get out of a chair without a forklift. A real Miss Dainty. I had to roll myself off the bed and then haul myself up by the bedpost. My stomach was so big I couldn't get food from the plate to my mouth without bumping into it. I couldn't cook without mixing my dress into the pot: the front of all my maternity dresses made me think I should wear a bib.

"Well, finally, after all the waiting and delays, the baby arrived. Of course, it was late, which was to be expected considering the plush accommodations. And it came the hard way, turned the wrong way, feet first, like it was trying to apply the brakes or something. And it was a boy. My husband was really happy. He even sold more cars than usual that week. He bought a gun. I stayed home, trying to figure out what I was supposed to do.

"All I had were some books the doctor gave me to read. Here they are." She patted her bag. "I should have known better than to believe anything my doctor suggested."

She pulled one of her books out of the bag, opened it to a page she wanted, and read: "'Babies like rocking motion and the sounds of lapping water because it reminds them of when they were carried aloft inside their mothers.'"

She put the book back in the bag. "*Aloft*—what kind of word is that? I should have known right away that someone saying 'aloft' had no help for me. But I went and played tapes of water sloshing. With the first sound of one wave lapping, he began to scream. Did I turn the water off? Did I stop rocking him? No.

"They said I should swaddle him, you know, wrap him up tight in receiving blankets." She pulled out another book. "It says, 'Bandaging arms and legs in on themselves in such a way as to restrict movement re-creates the womb and reassures the baby.'

"I don't know what happens to women when they become mothers that they buy into such garbage. Naturally my kid never liked being wrapped up so tight he couldn't twitch his nose. He was suffocating in all those blankets, but did I stop wrapping him up? Why were those blankets called receiving blankets? Was the baby received into this world by a blanket or by a mother? In my kid's case, he probably thought a blanket received him, the way this big pile was tied around him. I don't think my son liked his reception, and all the time I thought it was my fault."

She stopped and looked out the window for a minute. "My husband wanted to move to Florida for the better car market. I hate Florida. We moved. Money, you know.

"After being all wrapped up as a baby, when the kid could walk, he never stayed still. He was always on the go. The heat in Florida didn't slow him down a bit. He moved so fast, he didn't learn how to read. I tried to read him stories, nice slow stories. He yanked the book from my hands. He wouldn't eat with us and he wouldn't sleep at night and he wouldn't let me touch him. I was afraid I was going to hit him.

"I didn't ever hit him, but I was so afraid I started staying away. Staying away, making excuses—I'm to blame, all right, for what he turned into. I let him run all he wanted around the house because I was afraid I would hit him. I couldn't say to anyone, 'Hey, I want to kick my kid, what should I do?' I couldn't say, 'I'm living in a state I hate, with a car salesman whose business is good, and my son moves so fast I can't catch him.' I couldn't say, 'I don't know what to do.'

"Whatever I was feeling went on behind closed doors. I was supposed to love him no matter what. I was his mother. There was supposed to be a special bridge between us, all the books said so. So, where was it? I never knew the right thing to do for him. I just folded my hands in my lap and listened to my son making a disturbance in the other room.

"Finally he went to school for most of the day and I took a job to get out of the house. My husband wanted to have another baby. He said his business was good, we didn't need my income. My job at the warehouse wasn't much, but I didn't want to give it up and I didn't want another baby. I met a man who was bicycling his way around the country and laying over in Florida for a while. Every day I watched him run the forklift from my glass booth while I answered the phone. After a couple of weeks I started chasing him until he got the idea I wanted something. My husband got custody—I didn't even ask for it. After the divorce, I hung around Florida for a while, working at the warehouse, seeing the kid sometimes. But there wasn't much point. I've lived a lot of places, don't stay anywhere too long. Just keep moving. Haven't seen my son since I left." She suddenly broke off.

"The next stop is mine." And then she was gone, leaving me to ride to the end of the line.

Order

When she heard about my engagement, Mrs. Galloway weighed in with a story called "Order." It landed in my mailbox a few days after my bus ride.

A and B conducted their lives by making lists and then following them. Being busy people with C, D, and E to do and two children, f and g, A and B did not care to duplicate each other's efforts or waste time figuring out what A expected of B and B expected of A. Practicality was the bedrock of their marriage.

Over morning coffee, A made up a list for himself and a list for B, B made up a list for herself and a list for A, and then they cross-referenced. Items C, D, and E were familiar and long established, but each day offered new items H, J, and K to be incorporated. A and B were calmed when they set priorities; time was punctuated, meted out, apportioned. A knew how B would be occupied; B knew where A might be found if necessary. A and B headed to their cars and daily routines with a clear sense of C, D, E, f, g, H, J, and K.

At night, over supper, A checked off the completed items of the day's lists, saying, "There, C's done. D's done. E's done. What a relief!" B said, "H is done. J is done. K is done. F and g are safely home. What a relief!" Because unscheduled time made A and B nervous, they created a joint list of what could be accomplished with the evening before going to bed.

Even before A and B married, they made lists. Lists of the places they went on dates (they drew up a map), meals they ate (they collected menus), what B wore (wardrobe check), places A kissed B and places B kissed A, places where they had disagreements (ranked according to severity). They made lists of the order in which they should become engaged, marry, buy a house, have f, have g, buy a new car, redo the kitchen, refinance the house, and start a retirement plan.

Their list making was not confined to those they shared with one another. A and B each made lists for themselves alone. While A and B were engaged in C, D, or E, for example, X might preoccupy them—something off to the side, something they had forgotten or misplaced, some unfinished thing. B would keep a list of comments that upset her but to which she did not choose to respond; A wrote down the initials of people he would fire if promoted.

There were lists of an even more private nature. A, needless to say, did not show his to B, nor did B show hers to A. It was not unusual for lists to explode from their pens as sudden as short circuits.

A and B were legendary for their habit of lists. It was a joke among their circle of friends, L, M, N, O, P, and Q.

L would say, "I wonder what A and B are doing."

M would answer, "They're making a list." N, O, P, and Q would laugh.

Friends R, a divorce lawyer, and S, a marriage counselor, sometimes speculated that A and B's marriage would break down without lists.

In time, L, M, N, O, P, and Q began joking about the list making in A and B's presence. L, M, N, O, P, and Q never admitted the degree to which they themselves depended on lists. In response to the jokes, and as an experiment, A and B decided to stop making lists.

R and S cautioned, "Don't abruptly cease list making. We advise a gradual reduction."

I said, "It isn't like cutting out that bowl of ice cream after dinner, you know." But A, B, L, M, N, O, P, and Q didn't hear.

L, M, N, O, P, and Q eagerly awaited the results.

I said, "There's a thin line between order and breakdown." I was right. Without lists, A and B didn't know what to do with themselves. They walked from room to room, increasingly cranky. Irritability blossomed into discontent. A no longer knew what B expected. B no longer knew what A expected. Who was responsible for the dinner menu? Who would purchase the necessary groceries? Who would prepare the meal? And who would clean up afterward? Many evenings without dinner ensued.

A said to B, "I thought you would take care of it."

B said to A, "I thought you would take care of it."

And so they did nothing. A and B stopped having sex; it wasn't on a list.

Resentment set in. Was A responsible for collecting the trash and hauling it to the curb? A and B each waited until the garbage truck was a few houses away to see if the other would respond. At the last moment, A or B threw on clothes, yanked the bags out of the tins, and ran out front to see the truck rounding the corner and leaving their block. Returning to the house, A picked a humdinger of a fight with B, or B picked a humdinger of a fight with A.

Every act was open to question. Will A do C? Will B do C because A wants her to? Will A avoid C regardless of what B wants? A and B discovered that neither of them cared to do C, D, or E. Why must C be done? What will happen if neither A nor B does C?

L, M, N, O, P, and Q began to smell disaster. When R and S dropped over, A and B didn't answer the doorbell. Yelling could be heard. A and B became unreliable, failing to show up at social functions and never calling. A and B argued about whether they had agreed to show up. B thought A did very little and appeared directionless; A thought B was self-absorbed and unpredictable. Both thought C, D, and E were falling unfairly on their shoulders.

B said to A, "I no longer love you."

A said to B, "I no longer love you."

A and B together said, "Nothing is happening."

I noticed that the house was falling into disrepair. The rain gutters and downspouts hung from the roof, useless, and uncollected newspapers lay in the tall grass. "Is the house vacant?" I wondered.

A and B contemplated separation and felt compelled to examine the past as documented in boxes of old lists.

A asked B, "Why weren't we content to just think these thoughts?"

B asked A, "Why did we have to write them down?"

The emerging portrait of A and B's marriage wasn't pretty. Dirty socks, new toothbrushes. "Where is elevation?" they sighed. "Look at C. Look at D. Look at E. Disgusting!"

Not only were their daytime lives a mess, now they came to have nightmares. In A's nightmare, he is a young boy sitting at a picnic table with his relatives, T, U, and V, in the middle of a large field. Everyone at the table is turned to watch A's mother, W, walking toward them. The wind is blowing. W's dress wraps around her legs, impeding her. Cupped in her hands, as if the contents might spill, she carries a small piece of yellow notepaper. What is written on the paper? A letter? A strains to see. No, a list. A is afraid the wind is going to knock the list out of W's hands and hurl it across the field. No one will be fast enough to catch it. A thinks the list will tell him what to do. The wind is on the rise. He waits anxiously for W's arrival; she weaves through the grass.

When he wakes, A says to B, "No one will be fast enough to catch it."

In B's nightmare, there is a list, but she doesn't have it. She tries while tossing and turning to remember all the things written on the list. Each task is to be completed and crossed off before she wakes. Again and again B goes over the list she doesn't have, trying to remember exactly what is on it. Everything will be all right when I remember the list, she thinks. There is always one part she can't recall. She breaks into a sweat, her heart races.

When she wakes, B says to A, "Everything will be all right when I remember the list."

Sleepless, hungry, the house in ruins, ready to divorce, A and B agreed to go back to list making. However, they did not simply reactivate C, D, and E. Too much bitterness and recrimination had intervened. A and B had indeed discovered large deposits of resentment buried during the years of their smooth-running marriage. A and B produced lengthy lists of grievances. If A and B's marriage was to continue, new and different lists would have to be negotiated, in a different order and perhaps with side agreements listing those grievances never to be spoken of again. A and B agreed that periodically the lists would be reviewed by R and amendments considered. Further, A and B would seek counseling with S, both singly and as a couple. They drafted lists each could agree on separately and a list for what could be counted upon together. A and B agreed to agree to make the best of it, that is, to add Y for certain and if possible to continue all the way to Z.

Although there was no forgiveness, L, M, N, O, P, Q, R, and S said, "Welcome back."

I, being both in and out of this story, found it very hard to interpret.

Love

At the cleaning service, I worked with a woman who loved dentists, or at least had once been in love with the idea of them. She was my supervisor; she had started on the phones and worked her way up. She had the notion that I possessed the perfect mouth, with perfect teeth, and therefore was lucky in love. Nothing, be it my personal accounts of romantic disaster or the gap between my front teeth, dissuaded her from this view.

She was on a quest for the perfect mouth, which she thought would lead to love. I found this out one day when she stopped in front of my desk and spotted my engagement ring. She said, "You don't know what it's like not being born with perfect teeth. Your teeth are white and even; you don't even have fillings. And look, now you're engaged."

"I *do* have fillings."

"Unlike you, I have a history. Before I was in kindergarten, before I rode a bike, I wore an appliance. The first time my parents took me to the dentist—you know, when the kid gets her first toothbrush and smile sticker—my parents were presented with a long list of my defects. I inherited my upper jaw from my father and my lower jaw from my mother, which means my mouth is a battlefield. My upper jaw is recessive, too short and narrow, and my lower jaw is too long and prominent. Without correction, the dentist said, my chin would get longer and longer while my upper lip disappeared. You can imagine the joy in that news. I was a real mess, right from the start.

"The appliance was a failure. It was decided that nothing could be done but watch as my permanent teeth came in. After that, the problem could be attacked. Doing nothing as my teeth pushed through in the most helpless positions effectively killed my childhood. They angled through in every possible direction and at different heights. My jaws ached, it was so hard to chew. With every new tooth, my face looked more like a cubist portrait of betrayal, and my parents got separate beds."

The phone rang. I started to pick it up, but she said, "Let someone else answer it. Finally, intervention was warranted. I began wearing braces, on the top and bottom, to move toward what they called *alignment*. In those days, I heard a lot about alignment, that utopian condition of reconciliation between the warring lines of my mother's and my father's genetic pools. I have bitterly wondered why I had to bear the consequences of their ill-conceived intermingling, why their differences had to be so forcefully passed onto me. They told me I was the product of love, which didn't speak well for it. Every visit to the orthodontist I'd lay open my mouth as wide as I could, opening myself to pain, expected and inevitable pain. My face was a burning sky all along the fault lines of my cheekbones to my ears.

"With all the worry about the shape of my mouth, everyone forgot about my brushing. Until the age of twelve, I hardly brushed at all. Then at my checkup the dentist, who happened to be new to the office, young, and unusually handsome, discovered all my cavities. Up to then I had been handled impersonally by aged practitioners.

"That summer I spent every Tuesday morning having my teeth plugged with silver. I liked being worked on, opening my mouth as wide as possible for his hands to drill the farthest tooth. I liked being a patient. My mouth hurt, as it had before, but I was also exhilarated to have my cavities filled, two a week. The pain got all mixed up with the beautiful cleanliness of his hands and the shiny instruments his female assistant handed to him.

"His face came very close to mine, as you might imagine, so close I could see his smooth and warm skin, his lips, and inside his mouth to his teeth, his gums, and his tongue. We were almost lip to lip. Looking into his mouth over the drill as he looked into mine, I thought that pink was the color of love. His gums bloomed a healthy, robust pink. I thought of pink bassinets in the hospital, pink plastic baby bracelets with name, date, and birth weight, the pink insides of a rabbit's ear, the pink blur of a cut radish, salmon flesh, the pink of a worm in the sun, Shirley Temples and lobster, the pink veins, faintly etched, in the petals of a cherry blossom, the pink-dotted swiss of the bridesmaids' dresses at my sister's wedding, the pink satin ribbon running under my breasts and ending in a large bow at the back. As his mouth grew large, I imagined myself asking, 'Will you make my teeth perfect, will you love me?' I checked the Tuesday appointments off the calendar like stolen kisses."

I was grateful to have gone to Uncle James.

"But, of course, I am no longer twelve. I've always wanted two things—perfect teeth and perfect love. In search of them I've dated dentists endlessly. My address book reads like a Who's Who of the profession. Dentists are really artists at heart, misunderstood and feared by the public. Theirs is the art of maintenance and regularity. I've avoided the other professions, couldn't imagine sleeping with someone who didn't seriously brush and floss before going to bed. I could never turn out the lights and feel the particles of grist, the chewed remnants of the day, as his mouth touched mine. Little rags of veal, the nubs of corn. Oh no, my romantic life has been a modern-day quest of sorts, navigating my way from dentist chair to dentist chair.

"I haven't as yet found a dentist who will love me, nor has my mouth reached perfection. I'm twenty-eight and I haven't found the man who can fit his hands into my mouth and hold me. I'm discouraged. My apartment overflows with toothbrushes, Water Piks, mouthwashes, and a lifetime's supply of dental floss. I just don't have the storage space, so I've started giving the supplies away. Do you want a Water Pik?"

"No, thank you. I—"

"No one dentist satisfies me—I have to keep moving onto the next, and the next. I get tired of their chairs and the snappy reminders to brush and floss after every meal. At first I admire their teeth, their expertise, the way they say, 'I will fix you, I know how,' but the endless brushing doesn't end in love. I fall asleep in bed waiting for them to finish their dental routine. Of the discussions of hygiene I'm tired. Having to inflict it, they harden themselves against pain. The surgical precision of their lovemaking isn't what I wanted—the way they say *open*. I don't feel the necessary pain and the beauty when they enter me, and I don't feel the healing afterward."

The phone rang, but she was musing too deeply to notice. I picked the phone up and said, "Sisters, Inc. How may I help you?"

Faucet

I want to tell you about a terrible time I had. It isn't a story about a car wreck or the loss of my child. I didn't wake up with amnesia or married to my father. I wasn't kidnapped and kept bound and blindfolded for ten days in a toolshed before escaping and leading the police to my captors. It's not a storm piece about sailors riding out a typhoon; it wasn't ominously foretold by a barometer that dropped like a stone. It is about endurance and survival, but not in the snowy wilderness after an airplane crash, limbs broken, butting my way out of the wreckage with my head, only to have the helicopter carrying me to the hospital crack up too. No, it's about an experience I had in my kitchen.

(Sound of birds singing)

It was Saturday morning two weeks before the wedding, and my fiancé was off on errands. My first task was to wash the dishes from last night's dinner, my mother's old Wedgewood china she had sent me, piled in and around the sink. Cleanup was my job, since I didn't cook. My fiancé sometimes spoke fondly of dinners his wife had cooked, especially her cheesecake truffles.

It was a gloomy kitchen with dark cabinets and a deep red floor. I turned on the hot water and looked out the window while the water warmed up. I knew the color of the sky: it was blue, June blue, the kind of blue you wait for all winter. The garden was beautifully planted but hadn't been tended of late, and neglect was apparent in the backyard scene. The grass had grown up and toppled over on itself. The flower beds had become occupied territories, and nightshade besieged the trellises. Trimming and weeding were on today's list, and pleasant they would be, out in the fine day with the deep blue irises, and with the fragrant peonies and mock orange.

I stuck my finger under the spout to test the temperature of the stream and turned on the cold water to make it comfortable for washing. I had always liked the sound of it, water that is. I had stood at the sink many times and thought how the mind clarifies, washing dishes in water we no longer feel. We wash, the window swims before us, and we are gone.

(A phone rings)

Then the phone rang, and I put my hands on the faucet to turn off the water. The hot water on my left shut off easily, as water does in the normal course of things, with unheeded efficiency. But the cold knob, instead of stopping the flow, came off in my hand, valve and all—and water shot straight out into my face and chest at full pressure. I gave a little shriek of surprise at the assault, half-hearted because even the shriek was assaulted, drenched before it could get out of me. I got water in my nostrils and closed my eyes as if I might be blinded, and everything disappeared, including my ability to think. I stood stunned, unable for some seconds to register what had happened, the knob in my hand. I couldn't quite get straight what it was doing there; I no more expected it than I would expect an arm to detach at the shoulder when I shook someone's hand. Another time I might have examined the knob like some inscrutable lump at a garage sale, or given it a shake to see if it had loose innards like an old lightbulb, but water was spraying my face, and after a few seconds of dumb amazement I was soaked, my glasses dripping, and I couldn't see much of anything. Instead of making an examination, I screamed—I was far enough past the first shock to fully feel it and ready for a good yell. I have no idea what I screamed, only that I screamed for what felt like a long time. The blue day was all gone, and someone was leaving a message on the answering machine.

There couldn't have been more than a couple of seconds of screaming before I stopped and woke up to some sense of what had happened, aware that the knob was no longer resolutely anchored to the rest of the faucet, the kitchen sink nicely part of the house's plumbing, connected via incoming water mains and outgoing sewers to the neighborhood's and then whole city's system, and so on, to and from the sea. The knob was not in fact attached to anything, was its own item in my hand and could now, for example, be used as a paperweight. Once it sank in that the knob had come off, I realized that it might go back on. I tried to screw it onto the faucet, pushing against the hard stream jetting out from where the valve had gone, the water that close to the source almost a solid body in its force. The knob slid around with the eerie feel of two magnets pushed together at the wrong poles. I was taking a sea of water in the face, and the knob wouldn't screw on. I couldn't get it started. Water was accumulating on the floor, and I was sloshing in it. I could stifle the stream by pushing the knob on and holding it there with the strength of both hands. That kept the spray out of my face, but the second I loosened my grip or shifted my weight, the pressure forced the knob and water shot out into the kitchen again.

Now my mind was working hard. I knew that it was possible to cut off the water for the whole house. A shutoff existed somewhere, but where? Probably in the basement. I thought, This isn't my house, it's rented. If I let go to find the shutoff, the kitchen will flood, the water will ruin the wallpaper and linoleum, and I will be held responsible, even though it isn't my faucet. So I stood there, pressing the knob at just such an angle to keep the spray under control, if you could call it that, leaning over at an ungainly tilt, my neck already aching, trying to rest my head against the cabinet to the right of the sink to get some leverage.

Faucet

In a few minutes, my wrists felt brittle and thin and ready to snap. I decided I better call for help. I cried out. But not very loudly because it seemed futile and ridiculous. Who would hear me, who would come? The kitchen was small, and I was bounded on all sides by appliances and cabinets.

(A phone rings)

The phone was ringing, and there was a message. It was my mother.

"M., I've changed my mind. I think it should be the shrimp canapés, pickles 'n petals, and Gouda burst. Call me as soon as you can."

I wondered about calling someone. Whom would I call and what would I say? "Hello, this is an emergency, I can't turn my water off"? Can you call the police and say, "My faucet has fallen off, come quick"? Could I call the fire department to report, "I don't know how to turn the water off, it just keeps coming, please help"? Would the police or fire department answer such a request? Or would they think it a prank like the calls to liquor stores we made as kids: "Do you have Prince Albert in a can? Well, please let him out." Chances were good my crisis would merit the response we always got, a click on the other end of the line. Or maybe if a voice answered, it would say, "Madam, there are many women with faucets broken. You'll have to wait your turn." I managed to give a grim smile, and I congratulated myself on keeping my sense of humor.

I couldn't see out the window into the backyard because my glasses were fogged and sliding down my wet nose. But I thought I saw a blurred shape moving in the yard adjacent. I called and called. This time I meant it. I risked waving my left hand for a second before jamming it back on the knob. No one answered or came. Perhaps he didn't know how to interpret my calls, or perhaps there was no one there after all. At least an earthquake is over in a minute or two, I thought, and if you're not lying under rubble, you can shake your head over it with family and neighbors.

I was still holding the knob, but as the minutes went on, I was getting shakier and my wrists were burning and losing strength. The water was making headway, even beginning to shoot again. I could see the wall clock creep forward. I could not hold on indefinitely, and I had no idea when anyone would arrive to help me. I thought of bracing something against the knob, maybe a pan or dish. Nothing worked—the force of the water was too strong.

I was crying, which surprised me because I didn't cry much. Not a few tears you can brush away, but the ones that build and build to a high hysteria. I was crying in ways reserved for the dead; I was falling apart. It had happened so suddenly. A knob broken, and fifteen minutes later I was having a nervous break-down. I was sobbing, "Someone help me"—faintly—and then in a high-pitched scream. I knocked my head against the cabinet, screaming, "Is anyone going to come?"

I quieted down again and thought, this won't do. I imagined how I would be remembered, and my obituary flashed before me: "Woman Dies from Broken Faucet; Body Discovered When Water from Kitchen Bursts Out of the House in a Torrent." I rehearsed what my fiancé would say to those who asked how he had lost his bride-to-be just before the wedding. "Well, I lost her when the cold water faucet broke. It took an hour. Imagine if it had been the hot water faucet: then it would have been a matter of minutes. Too bad she didn't know where the shutoff valve was. All women should learn where the shutoff valve is."

Half an hour after the knob fell off, and I thought, This is my life, this is it—standing here holding on the knob of the cold water faucet while outside there is a numbingly blue sky. I dropped a hand free and broke all the dishes in the sink. I broke all the dishes in the dish rack. I broke everything I could get my hand on—the glass jar of brown sugar, the canisters of flour, sugar, creamer, and cornstarch. I would have broken more but I ran out of things to break. The sugar and creamer oozed along the counter, pooled in the burners of the stove, and ran down into the oven, dripped in a thick stream down the cabinets and onto the floor, the texture of gravy. Pieces of china and glass, large and small, washed into the stream. My mother always said I didn't take proper care of things. I guess she was right. I felt for the moment beyond imploring or tears. What else, what else? I've broken everything I can and I'm standing in water mixed with flour and sugar and pieces of my mother's old china.

A broken faucet is a domestic shipwreck, except that there is no warning, no clue to detect that the faucet is going to break. At no time did I ask why it was happening to me. At no time did I think it an unlikely fate. Once it happened, it seemed what I expected, if not deserved. Whatever domestic fates are in the world, they were getting even with me, showing me who's who. Did I think I could escape from the kitchen my whole life? Ha, Ha! they say—we've shown you. I gave another grim smile.

I had once again managed to force the knob farther back onto the valve and the water had abated, but the water pressure was building again. I leaned into the sink, summoning all my reserves. I had been standing at the sink nearly all my life, about forty-five minutes.

(A phone rings)

Another phone call. The answering machine switched on, and I could hear the muffled sound of someone saying hello. I didn't want to know who it was—the thought of understanding the words stabbed me in the heart. I felt another hysterical wave rising, and this time there was nothing to break but myself. I shot out of the wave, poised above a void, lifted clean out of the water with a quiver running through me. As I surmounted one wave, there was another behind it even more desperate than the last. Something threw its weight on me, trying to pin me down, deep-swimming. Never for a moment could I shake myself clear of the water. I saw in myself the ominous signs of exhaustion. I felt that I was no longer struggling. The water was thick as gravy and black.

My fiancé came in the front door. I called, "Help me, please,

please, help me." My voice was swollen and unmoored. Perhaps he noticed something strange in it, wracked, unsteady, and mournful. He took his time getting to me, as if he must sail from a far horizon over the black silk sea. When he got to the kitchen door, he stopped. My voice broke and sank, and my fiancé saw what had happened. He reached under the sink and turned off the valve. The water slowed to a drip. I dropped the knob. I couldn't move, inclined as I was toward the missing water.

"What happened?" He stared at me. "Why didn't you just shut off the water?"

I couldn't begin to tell him. I went upstairs and lay down on the bed.

He stayed downstairs, muttering bitterly, picking out the pieces of china and glass and throwing them into the trash. He played the phone messages. The kitchen shone far below my lightheadedness. My hands were going through the old mechanical, bloodless motions of handwashing. My hands will not stop going through the steps. There is no body attached to the hands, no face. The hands are absolutely clean, suspended in air, with a life of their own. I knew I wouldn't have to wash my hands for a long, long time.

(Sound of birds singing)

Voice

They take away all your clothes and lock them in a closet whose location is unknown.

They take away your purse and everything in it and lock it away. This is a relief; I will not reclaim it.

They ask you to fill out a form, an inventory of everything they took away. The items are few, numbingly few, not much more than I was wearing: jeans, shirt, socks, sandals, jacket, scarf. In the purse: wallet, one paper clip, keys, lipstick, lists.

They give you a smock, like the one I wore when I was learning to wash hands. It ties in two places at the back and flaps open easily whenever I move. Why are there only two ties in the back that flap open when I move? Why have they not given me a gown that closes all the way up and down, perhaps with snaps in the front, easy to reach? Why am I not dressed more properly? A pair of blue pajama bottoms that tie in the front. These are too tight in the calves.

They give no towels. I ask for a toothbrush and toothpaste. A plastic pail appears with small soap, baby powder, mouthwash, a tiny box of Kleenex, a toothbrush and paste. No hairbrush or shampoo or deodorant or hand lotion.

They have put me in a room with two beds. I am in the number 2 bed, number 1 is empty. The light over the bed doesn't work, nevertheless I am in the number 2 bed. No one occupies number 1, whose overhead light works. What do I need light for? A curtain can be pulled to encircle each bed.

There are no phones in the room. The cord could be put to a

harmful purpose, and screens have been locked over the windows. There are no hangers, and the beds are narrow, white, and made up with something other than sheets. The walls are off-white and bare.

It is very late and it has been a long day. As I pass from one department to another, I must fill out inventories and questionnaires about my medical history, my family's medical history, questions about depression, anxiety, sleep disorders, eating patterns, do I hear voices. All the questions are the same, but each department has its own form.

In the last department a man in his twenties, at the end of his shift, asks the questions from the form on his clipboard. "Age?"

"Nineteen. Dial M. for marriage."

He looks at me askance for a few seconds, bent over his clipboard. "Do you want to hurt yourself?"

I say nothing.

He looks at his watch. He goes back to his form and circles *DNR*. "Do you want to be alive?"

I say nothing. He circles *DNR*.

"Do you feel helpless—excuse me, I mean *hope*less?"

DNR.

He puts away his clipboard and stands up. "Would you like some saltines or water?"

DNR.

He goes away to get the saltines. When he comes back, I ask, "Are you going to instruct me about washing my hands?"

"Do you *want* me to?" he replies, looking at his watch.

"It's complicated."

"How so?"

"Well, the faucet broke in my kitchen. Actually, it wasn't my kitchen, it was in my fiancé's kitchen."

"Yes," he says, "faucets sometimes break. But ours here work if you want to wash your hands. And yours can be fixed."

"My fiancé did, when he came home. I didn't know where the shutoff valve was. And I don't think I'll need to wash my hands for a long time. I thought I should mention this."

"Ah, the shutoff valve is very important. What else has been happening?"

"I couldn't sort things out like my Uncle James."

"Uncle James?"

"He sorted his laundry into piles. But he died alone. And I was afraid there'd be no love if I didn't get married."

"Are you getting married?"

"My mother wants me to. Like washing hands. Did I mention I won't have to wash my hands?"

"Yes, you did. That point is clear. Now you were telling me about getting married."

"My fiancé wanted to get married for . . . I suppose because he didn't want to lose me. And I couldn't say no, at least not in any way they'd understand. I guess I wasn't ready to lose him either."

"An old story." He's writing a lot on his clipboard.

"That's what Uncle James said. What kind of woman am I?"

He finishes his sentence on the clipboard. "What kind of woman do you think you are?"

"I've been feeling as if a wheel was turning to lift me toward marriage, yet as the motion was going forward, I was going backward, disappearing. I've been having a dream lately about my wedding dress. Do you want to hear it?"

"A dream. Yes, please tell me."

"I decide to sew my own wedding gown, an odd choice if you knew my history. My wedding gown is the A-line with the problem zipper in the back."

"A-lines. I've never heard of them." He is writing on his clipboard.

"Oh mister, let me tell you, A-lines are very real. They're as real as anything in this world, as real as Jell-O."

He writes *Jell-O*.

"I go to a fabric store, buy some very sheer material, a pattern, and start sewing. Next I'm at the wedding ceremony, and the A-line unsews itself until by the kiss it's the pieces of the pattern I began with. The shoulder flaps fall down to my breasts, the seams gape, not all at once but bit by bit, all through the vows, and at last the zipper in the back pulls away from the dress. I try to hold myself together, but the groom is unaware of the unraveling going on next to him. Don't you think that's important?"

"What's important? The zipper or the groom not noticing?"

"Well both, but mainly that the groom doesn't notice what's going on right next to him."

"I see. Well, go on." He writes *zipper* down.

"When he tries to slip the ring on my finger, he notices. I can't extend my arm. It's clutching the shoulder flap over one breast, and the other hand is cranked behind my back, at a severe angle, gripping the sides of the dress where the fabric has become unmoored from the zipper. At this point, I just let go of the whole mess, the effort of holding myself together is too much, and I let my sack of penance fall to the feet of the altar.

"Sack of penance—what are you referring to?"

"My dress, that's what I'm talking about."

"Your dress. I thought you might be referring to the mess."

"Look, I was standing before the gathered congregation in my slip. I might as well have been naked. And I wake up choking."

He stares. "Hmm, yes, I see. Would you like more saltines?"

"Yes. I don't want to wake up and find Miss Needlebaum. There's got to be something sweet along the way. It can't be all Jills and Needlebaums."

"Who?" He doesn't wait for an answer. He goes to get the saltines.

When he comes back, he says, "Let me ask you: Do you hear voices?"

Last night I dreamed I died. I was in a huge boat, not a sailboat or a motorboat—a long wood boat with oars and seats for twelve. Everyone had an oar. The boat gleamed the way wood that has been carved and whittled looks bleached and clean. On shore people waved good-bye, but it was too dark to see their faces or know who they were. Overhead the sky was dark too, violently purpled, thunderous, with fast-moving clouds racing closer and closer. The water churned, choppy and dark. Only the boat was illuminated. Suddenly someone shouted, *Anchors away!* and *Pull!* We were shoved away from shore, and we dipped our oars in unison. *Pull harder, harder, harder,* someone shouted again. We were cutting through the water with incredible force. I had never felt such force and exhilaration. I thought the boat was going to lift up out of the water and fly. I was at the bow, absorbed in pulling, and never looked behind, never turned to see who else rode the boat. I woke up in the middle of the night, feeling the wind and water on my face, the chill of lake water, my chest heaving.

"I'm tired. Just leave the saltines, okay?"

After he leaves, I dim the light on the other bed, bed number 1. Why didn't I ask to be in bed number 1 when there's no one else in the room and my light doesn't work? There isn't much to see. The screens block any view from the windows, inside or out. I'm on the ninth floor, so no one could see me even if I stood at the window. I am invisible.

I'm exhausted but can't sleep. Do I hear voices? What kind of question is that? Of course I hear voices—but not the kind he thinks I hear.

I wouldn't come downstairs. That's why I'm here.

I didn't behave angrily. It would have been better if I had. I didn't break anything, but then I had already broken just about all the dishes and glassware. I was very quiet. I was dissolving, as I always feared I might. I didn't put up a fight when my fiancé said to take me to a clinic. My estimate of him did sink, but this last dip wasn't too perceptible.

The phone rang and he answered it. "Well, first the faucet broke. That's right, I said the faucet. In the kitchen." Pause. "No, she couldn't screw it back on. I wasn't home." Pause. "About an hour. It was the cold water." Silence.

A bed with hospital corners, tiny flat pillows like communion wafers.

Do I hear voices? So much instruction. How will I get it right?

And now here you are, Ginger Baker. I don't know why I'm thinking of you. Why have you entered my room, my sick room? I never even knew you. I'm all grown up, or trying to be. What have you to do with my life?

You were the friend of my sisters; you never even said hello to me. You're like a cigarette someone can't put out. You were my mother's example of what not to be, of what can go awry in a girl's life. I have trouble separating *you* from what my mother made of you. And yet I see you always a little to the left of her example. Who would my mother have pointed to if you didn't exist?

She started with your name: "Who would name their daughter *Ginger*? It's a name for a small yapping dog or a bleached-blond stripper, not a name for a nice girl in a small town." Your name did not bode well for a bright future, and that's what my mother wanted for her daughters, that's what most mothers want for their daughters, isn't it? *A bright future.* My mother was not unusual in her desires. If you had a daughter, isn't that what you would want for her? It seems perverse to not want a bright future. After all, who would want its opposite—*a dark past*? But what is a bright future? Is it the same for every girl? My mother's bright future was my dark past.

What my mother meant by bright future was for her daughters to be well married. Well married meant well provided for. Well provided for meant married to a husband who made a good living that was secure and dependable. Good living meant that her daughters wouldn't have to work or have ambitions for themselves, that they would be taken care of. We could live free of wanting. Of private disaster, she never spoke.

Perhaps my mother would say she wanted her daughters to live happy lives, that we might not experience the loss she underwent. But she would never speak of that loss. Because she would not speak of her private fears and sufferings, by happy I understood my mother to mean married and in repose. But I never wanted to be in repose; I wanted to be pitched like an acrobat through the air, like the girl who did flips on the trampoline. I wanted to think of my sisters and myself as budding, blossoming, falling to seed, and budding all over again. There would be seasons and cycles of change.

When speaking of you, my mother didn't specify the bad that would come, just that there would be an absence of ease. My sisters understood better than I; it was self-evident, apparently. I could not see the connection my mother drew between your name and your life. After all, my name suggested a funeral march. But apparently others no longer viewed your future as a matter of speculation; your life was a done deal. You had already gone bad. You dropped out of high school and had a baby. Fran and Gwen visited you at first, then no one mentioned your name. I wondered what became of you, and then I forgot you until today. Perhaps you had a bright future after all. Who knows? It's possible. Perhaps you had a beautiful daughter despite the dark past. Or because of it.

Ginger Baker, were you riding the long boat? Were we rowing together, did we share in the long rowing to the future? Was it you who shouted *Pull?*

Balance

Dear Reader, I married him.

But it was a mistake. Why would you do that? You knew nothing good could come of it.

I know, I know. The process was too far along to stop. I wanted to stop, but it had been set in motion a long time ago. Sometimes it isn't enough to see that you're making a big mistake; sometimes you have to go ahead and make it, to live it and carry it in your bones.

It's an unpleasant fact but true, some weddings are mistakes.

Some births are mistakes. Some children are born to parents who don't love them or can't love them for complicated reasons of their own that the children spend their lives trying to understand. What they will know is that the only way to right that mistake is to look for love elsewhere as best they can. That is what I set out to do. I set out to create a life of my own. The relations with my family never did sort themselves out; they were never transformed into something positive or redeeming.

You're getting yourself all worked up. Was that what the marriage was supposed to do? I mean transform relations?

I guess.

What was it like? The wedding.

A damp affair, as you might expect. Damp because it rained the whole day. The few gathered sat under umbrellas; my knot of violets slumped. My mother's friends tried to rally her by saying, "A light rain is a blessing, a blessing."

But the rain was not so light, maybe.

It was a downpour.

Was it a big wedding?

At least it was small. My professor lost a goodly number of his friends when he linked up with me. Our union destroyed much in its path. His family had little enthusiasm for a second wedding—the first hadn't been that long ago, and its memory was still fresh. My parents invited only loyal friends who had experienced troubles with their own children and wouldn't be too haughty. Looking out at the rows of rented wooden chairs sitting forlornly in the newly mown grass slowly filling up, I saw more flower girls than guests.

What about the ceremony?

I smiled grimly at first.

The ring?

Let's just skip it.

That's it? Then it was over?

An end predictable to all. At the reception my brothers-in-law made bets that the marriage wouldn't last a year. And they were right.

No, I mean then the wedding was over.

Well, there was the reception. About forty minutes in, I began to cry. My mother said, "Tears of joy, that's what she's crying."

I like the part when the bride tosses her bouquet.

We did that. I did that at the wedding.

When I was small, I used to accompany my mother and sisters to weddings—daughters of my mother's friends who were getting married and then friends of my sisters who were getting married. I didn't like them a bit except for that part, the bouquet thrown into a sea of women and all the girls intent on catching it. I didn't understand that the one who caught it would be the next to get married. It was just a fun game, the only lively part, and I liked flowers. I used to wiggle my way into the crowd—because I was small and short, I had an advantage. I could sneak past others, insinuate myself closer without anyone paying attention. I'd get myself into a good position, and then when the bride made the toss I'd leap into the air with precision timing and snatch that bouquet out of some poor girl's waiting hands. I liked when the bouquet sailed through the air and I sailed up to meet it. The flowers and I suspended over a staircase, all that momentum—it was like doing a flip on a trampoline. That was a happy moment. I developed a reputation after a couple of weddings when I departed with the catch, like a prize fish, and my mother stopped taking me or held me to her in another room when the toss took place. I recognized the bad feeling I had created even if I didn't understand it.

I didn't see much feverish desperation to catch my dying violets.

Then there were the photos.

As the official wedding photo my mother chose a morose headshot.

Official?

The one she hung next to the wedding photos of Fran and Gwen. It hangs today as we speak. I am bent down, and my hair has fallen forward, like a hood around my face. People who see it are embarrassed; they note, almost involuntarily, how young and sad I appear, that is, what they can manage to see of me. It's one of the saddest photographs I've ever seen.

Maybe it's the contrast that's embarrassing.

Fran and Gwen were every inch traditional brides, fulfilling every conventional expectation of what a bride is supposed to be. The culmination of their becoming women, the moment they had prepared themselves for. My photograph memorialized the beginning of the end.

So how did it end? I see you walking out of the house on the first snowfall of the year. There would have been a fight, a bad one along the same old lines, and you would leave. You strip off your ring.

Wearing it, I would develop a rash, a terrible red rash. And then I'd scratch it until all the skin flaked away, leaving a red angry band. In fights, of which there were many, I'd twist it off my finger with difficulty and hurl it into the night sky. After most fights I'd be able to retrieve it, having a fairly short throw, although it would be dented and nicked.

After years of married life, it would have looked like an old hubcap.

Eventually there came a time when I threw it somewhere from which there was no return. I threw it down a drain.

It teetered for a second on the grate, then clink clink clink, down the drain. Arrivederci marriage!

Later my husband had it annulled so he could marry a Catholic girl.

I like the word "annulled."

Futures

The city was having its annual May Day celebration. Traffic was blocked off and the streets were filled with tents and booths, and singing minstrels roamed. Gwen was visiting. We bought pierogies and munched and strolled. And then we saw a sign saying, Straight Ahead, Mrs. Draper, Fortune-Teller Extraordinaire.

"Let's go see the fortune-teller," said Gwen.

Great. A dimly lit room with a dark-haired woman dressed in the outlandish garb of a gypsy behind beaded curtains. "I doubt any living soul can see my future," I answered. "I believe in fate. And fortune plays no part in either."

Gwen hitched her purse higher on her shoulder. "What's the difference? Fate, future—they're all the same. Let's go and have some fun."

At least, I thought, there may be incense or spice in the air.

We found the tent and entered. On the other side of a card table sat a frumpy old woman dressed in a loose flowered print dress, a handkerchief tucked in the belt, and with multiple chins much lowered by gravity. When we came in, she sprayed whiffs of Glade from a can sitting on the ground behind her.

The woman peered at me as if she couldn't quite see me through the thick mist, and she moved heavily in her chair. She raised an arm with extra flesh and motioned Gwen to take the chair opposite hers.

She began to massage the palm of Gwen's hand and said, by way of explanation, "I need to get to know your hand before I can begin." Looking at me, but asking Gwen, she said, "Is this your first time?"

"No," Gwen said, "it isn't."

I couldn't contain myself. "You mean to say you have had your fortune read multiple times? Does it change?"

The woman kept massaging. "Who is your friend?" she asked.

Why couldn't she ask me directly? I was standing right there.

"My sister," Gwen said. "She believes in fate, not fortune. And she can really be a drag sometimes."

"Hmm," the woman said, turning to concentrate on Gwen. "Tell her there's a difference, but she has to believe."

"Believe in what?" I interrupted, irritated that she wouldn't direct her remarks to me.

"Believe that the skin you wear can be discarded, and that you must let it go. Your life depends upon it. And now," she concluded, "you must leave while I look into your sister's hand."

I walked outside and mused on what Mrs. Extraordinaire had said. I didn't go anywhere, for I had no idea how long it took to read someone's palm. Instead I leaned my ear against the thick canvas, trying to hear what the woman was saying. I couldn't make out a thing.

What happens when you seek your fortune and find it? I didn't think my fortune would turn up like the lost keys I searched for everywhere and eventually gave up hope of finding only to stumble upon them when I in cleaning pulled off the pillows of my couch. In the weeks after their loss I felt my life wouldn't be right until I found them. That odd feeling of knowing they were *somewhere*. Where could they have vanished? I thought if I found them, my life would click into place. But their return brought no realignment.

I didn't think it was like my grandmother's ring that I had lost. It vanished, never to be found. Could my fortune be like that? Did I throw it away or misplace it? Had it been lost? It wouldn't turn up like a lost key. The trouble with my fortune was of an entirely different order.

Gwen emerged.

"Well? What did she say?"

"All I can say is, it isn't always *in* the saying."

"What are you talking about? That's why we came."

"It's also about forgetting." And she gave me a push inside the tent.

I sat down and stretched my hand across the table, reluctantly. I said, "The only person who could see my future was my sister, and she's dead. I believe in fate. Fortune plays no part in either."

She looked at me calmly, and her eyes sharpened as if a mist were clearing. Then back to the hand. "What a small hand," she said, "no bigger than a child's." She turned it over and straightened the fingers, one by one. She pulled each firmly away from my palm and rubbed her finger inside my wrist.

"This reminds me of drawing blood," I said. "They can never find a vein. My veins run deep in the underground of my body, difficult to access, leery of surfacing. I'm sure I'm a difficult case."

"Really?" she said. "Well, we won't have that problem with your hand."

Now it was my turn. "Really?"

"No, never in my career have I seen such a written-upon hand. But still a little blurry, like a hand beneath the water. But don't worry, it's not a sheet of ice." She bent over my hand. "Ah, there we go."

"Tell me what you see."

"You are the girl who walked on tiptoe because your mother was lying down with a headache, who played outside in all weather so as not to fray your mother's tattered nerves and suggested meals your mother never cooked. You are the girl whose father expected you to take care of your mother."

I felt queasy, as if a most unappetizing meal had been set on my plate.

"You are the daughter who in a group of daughters listened and remembered everything. You are the girl other girls' boyfriends wanted. You are the girl who pretended not to care. Tom, Dick, or Harry were all the same to you, at the window, on the phone, in the car, at the door. Or so you pretended. You are the girl to whom others confess their secrets, having many secrets of your own."

As if tomatoes had been set on my plate. I interrupted. "You're telling me my past. I want to know my future."

"If you aren't careful, your past will be your future," she said, and she rapped my hand sternly against the table.

"Ouch! What did you do that for?"

"Listen, isn't that what you think your future will be? You think you will have no life of your own, am I right?"

Softly. "This is the price I must pay."

"Pay for what? Being alive?"

"Yes, for being alive."

"Now listen very carefully," she said. She was holding both my hands and stroking them with her thumbs. "If you want a future, you must forget. You must find a balance between remembering and forgetting, holding on and letting go. You can't do it all at once, all one way and then all the other. You can't *always* say yes or *always* say no. You must be flexible, acrobatic. I can tell you this—you are a swimmer of distances."

"How do you know this about me?"

"We're all adrift, dearie. Some of us struggle, and some of us let go."

I was still shaky. "No one would believe me if I told them what just happened."

"You're right, dearie, no one will believe you. Now listen just a little longer. This is the future I see when I hold your hands: In your house you will keep the windows open, even in winter, even in rain. Sometimes when it is raining you will stand at the window looking out, as your mother did. You will recall yourself, like a falcon bound with a heavy cord. But now you will be free, untethered. And ah! here is a child, pulling herself up to take her first steps."

She let go of my hands after giving them one last pull. She raised the arm with extra flesh and waved in a friendly way for me to go. "Your sister's waiting."

Before I was out of the tent, whiffs of fresh Glade were clearing the air for her next customer.

Bouquet

I lost everything that had been given to me, and I was glad. I set off on my own, saw many cities, and finally stayed in Seattle, on a coast far from my birthplace, to do some work, now that I was past twenty and beginning to form words on my own.

There I met my second husband, both of us thousands of miles from where we began in rooms where we were silent and alone. He had left a trail of partings in his wake; I had flown with the stars to the sea. Uncle James had asked, *If it's safe, can it be love?* It was a studied courtship full of profound transformations. This second time, it was enough that I did not fear the loss of love if I refused.

In the afternoon, with two friends as witnesses, we were married at City Hall. Neither of our families attended the ceremony. It was agreed that we were not marrying our families, though we admitted that they had turned to blood within us.

Our daughter, Lily, believes we were married on a bus. We weren't. We were married at City Hall, but we did ride the bus home. This part confuses her, and no matter how many times I correct her, she insists we were married on a bus in Seattle.

My niece sent me a wedding bouquet—a big bunch of yellow daisies with shiny black centers. It was a bouquet a child would choose, large and composed of flowers she might see growing in her front yard or in a wild field down the street, not an assortment of staged blossoms in the florist's icebox.

We picked up the bus downtown and took our seats at the back. Two in the afternoon on a Friday, and the bus was half full. When it stopped at our block, we walked down the aisle. My husband of one hour went first, and I followed, carrying my bouquet before me in time-honored fashion. He got off and stood on the curb. I hesitated by the driver, and then tossed my wedding bouquet to the passengers behind.

Not pausing for the likes of thrown bouquets, the bus pulled out and made its labored way down the street. A chaos of passengers rose up from the seats and stirred into the aisle, trying to catch the yellow daisies in midair. Flowers flashed like bus stops: bouquets I had aggressively snagged as a girl, bouquets my mother with her arm kept me from catching, limp violets that, listlessly tossed, had fallen into the grass before girls in rain-soaked dresses could catch them.

I'll never know who caught this bouquet. Perhaps it fell into the lap of an old man sleeping. Or perhaps a young girl got off at her stop and walked home clutching yellow daisies. She climbs the steps to her house and tells her parents how she came to be carrying such a bunch of flowers. They don't believe her. They are sure there is some other explanation.

Vinegar

To honeymoon we rode a ferry from Seattle and then boarded a bus that rocked us along the hedgerows of the coast to the quiet village of La Push. We settled our few belongings into our cabin and hiked over to the beach. Along the edges of the wheatfields ran sand dunes that took us softly down to the shore. I descended, my husband following, to find a few dogs and their owners, two children searching for shells in the mud-flats, one family moored behind windscreens. I stretched out at the foot of the dunes, a low bank of sand behind me tumbled with gorse, carrot root, and heather. Behind me, sloping down to the rock cliffs bordering the beach, a tractor slowly mowed the field; up and down the tractor inched, turning the cut field a paler gold than the uncut. It was a straw field, blond, knee-high, even. Squares of straw were blocked off by hedges, built with stones piled on their sides like books stacked on a shelf. A woman drove the tractor. I could ride a tractor, I thought, settle down to a life of farming. There are many lives I could live. After the woman mowed one row, she baled the hay with a deft turn of the fork, row after row into quick bales of hay. A dog accompanied her, following her down the rows, stopping when she stopped, moving when she moved.

I was tired from our journey, lay back, and would have fallen asleep right away but for the stutter of the low-veering gulls that like memories passed over one by one and infrequently, then skimmed up the dunes and disappeared, while the waves that rustled up the shore, and the heat of the sun, and the wind in which they plied their wings called me back. A young girl, bundled into the car with my father, bound for Hawk Mountain, on a Saturday morning in late summer. Rare it was when he took me on such a trip, just the two of us. We climbed a little trail to the top, where my father singled out one hawk, who idled above foothills too scorched to scour for prey, her wings open, and open forever, and at her turning like leaves shed in a motionless sky. Her solitary state struck me as my own, and I wondered how long she could hang, buoyed only by her own prowess. How much of myself could I conserve on so little? There was no comfort in numbers. But one must have many memories, each one different from the others. One must also be able to forget them from time to time.

I had never seen such clean gulls. Their bellies were pure white, their wings like gray ribbons edged in black that a child might try to fly on holiday, fresh and light in the air. No ragged numbers scavenged: there was nothing, absolutely nothing, to beg or plunder. The beach was beautifully clean, like new flowers opening in the morning, where the two children were burying themselves in sand far down the shore, my husband going off for a walk, the sand kicking up behind his feet. A little island sat offshore, as if waiting for me to swim out to it. What would I do once I had reached it? Make a wish? Like Lake Miranda and the last-night wish, when we campers sent our hope across the water, carried by a drifting candle. The wishing candle was made from a thin wooden disk, sliced from the trunk of a small tree. On one side, the camper counted out from the center the number of rings to match her age and there wrote her name in a dye that would not soon be washed away by water. On the other side she placed a fern and then dripped wax to hold the candle and fern in place. Sometimes I added a light remembrance of summer, a lock of my true friend's hair, or a pale blue flower, or written words of resolution and hope. On the last night, we sat around a bonfire on the circles of logs by the lake, singing the songs we had learned, until the dark was full. Then one by one each girl walked down to the shore, lit her candle, set it afloat and, as it met the lake, made a wish. If, carried by wind and currents, it washed up on the eastern shore the next morning, the wish would come true. Or so the tradition went.

The wind was picking up and lifting the gulls harder away from me.

My last year at Camp Miranda, the summer my mother insisted I carry on the tradition and work on the waterfront as Helen had—to learn, I supposed, responsibility—I was put in charge of preparing the ceremony for the last night of camp.

I wanted a floating fire on the lake. I built a raft, lashing logs together with strong rope. I soaked the lengths of log in kerosene, then nailed them to the raft to form a frame. Inside went the firewood, to be set ablaze by the framing logs. There were problems with every stage of the design, and I feared my vision of the burning lake was not going to be realized. The raft wanted to sink, and at one point I thought I'd have to swim underneath, as in a dream one moves in impossible ways, keeping it afloat.

A dream of waves.

On the last night the campers took their places, singing around the fire. I watched the torches spew their light upward. Once the night had come, the girls carried their wishing candles down to the dock, where they lit them and set them going on the journey across the lake. I felt the gathering of their wishing.

I started the raft afire, the flames jumping high above the water. I hoped the campers would see how it warmed the cold lake. I loosed the ropes that tied up our raft and sent it offshore. A giant candle, it floated behind the others, hundreds now on the slow current. I made a wish, the sort of wish it takes a whole life long of waiting and gathering to fulfill.

I don't know how long I slept. Perhaps years had passed, and I had been washed up mysteriously here. The beach had widened as the tide ebbed; swaths of wet sand, shiny and gray, snaked across it and disappeared. Dogs ran in the mudflats to smell each other, small children were digging in inch-deep water. I saw my husband standing above me. I didn't actually see him because the sun was too strong. I felt him. It's often like that, I can't see him clearly even when the light is weak. He is someone I feel before he comes into focus.

"You're burning," he said and brushed the sand from the backs of my legs.

"I fell asleep. When I woke up, I didn't know where I was."

"Do you remember now?" He dropped down beside me, brushed more sand from my legs.

When I first met him, I noticed his hands, for they were ceaselessly fitful. A man of gestures, he spoke with his hands. I spent a year observing them before I felt their touch. If someone in that first year had said, *You'll come to love those hands*, I would have scoffed. I thought I'd have to overcome them for the rest of him. They were not beautiful to look at. They are disproportionately small. The fingers were stubby and thick, while he is tall and smooth. They were the prematurely creased hands of a different man, an old man who had spent his life in manual labor. He knew they were off-putting, but he didn't hide them. He wondered how he got them, where they came from. Nothing prepared me for the heat and strength of them—the feel of sunbaked mud, closefitting and earthy, the memory of roads in unknown places. They were powerfully alive, the spirit of a young man inside their cracked skin.

When he touched me, it was a hot summer night in July. I asked him if he wanted to take a walk. It was dark, and the temperature was just beginning to drop. The insects bit me, through my shorts, behind my knees, around the ankles, even the tops of my feet. He had not received one single bite. His skin was too tough, he said. When we came home, my legs burned. We were in the kitchen, the blinds half-drawn, the windows open, one small lamp on the table lit.

"Sit down," he said. Then he began to ransack my poorly stocked cabinets.

"What are you looking for, perhaps I can help?"

He didn't respond. He found what he was looking for. "Ah,

good thing you like salads." He pulled a small bottle from the top shelf.

"Vinegar–what are you going to do with that?"

Again he said nothing. He pulled a chair in front of mine and sat down. He took one of my legs in his hands and rested it across his knee, then shook some of the vinegar from the bottle out onto his hands, just tiny drops, and lightly rubbed my leg. My legs were hot; his hands were hotter; they were always hot even in the dead of winter. He rubbed first my lower calves, then the back of my knees–that indentation like an artichoke heart or the flesh of a cherry under the skin. He pushed up my shorts to cover the upper parts, and began rubbing the vinegar into my flesh. I closed my eyes. Again and again he shook the bottle; sometimes he sprinkled it directly onto my leg, sometimes pouring the vinegar into his hands first. The hot dark came in through the windows, and the vinegar took away the sting. The clean smell rose from my legs, rose from his hands. He soothed first one leg and then the other; he took almost everything that had been away, massaging his way to the very center of me, to that part where later in childbirth I would feel pain.

Like all the wishing candles floating on the slow current of Lake Miranda gathered into one candle, one wish.

Plots

There are many gardens; some are realized, some are coming to realization, some reside in the mind's desire—secret gardens, psychic gardens, labyrinths, sanctuaries.

We bought a modest house in an old, close-knit neighborhood with sidewalks where, in good weather, people gather to chat. The house has a sad history the neighbors related when we asked why our small upstairs bedroom appeared to have been abandoned: a marriage had disintegrated after the sudden death of an infant. We, too, thought the room a perfect nursery, overlooking the side and back yards, a young child's size, intimate, and there our daughter spent her first night at home. Any house of age must have its sad histories. Many want a new house that no one has ever lived in, like a blank slate. I could never live in such a house. Even in bad weather, in thunderstorms and rain, I keep the windows open a crack. Sometimes I stand at the window, staring out, and recall myself like a falcon wearing a heavy hood. But now I am free, untethered.

The house is without a functioning kitchen. Several burners on the stove don't work, and the refrigerator closely resembles a toy. The seams in the linoleum floor long ago unsealed themselves, and the edges curl upward like a sneer; anyone who enters unaware is likely to trip. I love the kitchen; it suits me perfectly; I enter seldom. I am a kitchen ghost. My attitude toward food is, less is more. I like what I can buy and eat immediately, or by ripping open the bag or screwing off the lid: dried apricots and raisins, fresh fruit, nuts, donuts, crackers, cheese, pickles, ice cream. I don't like dishware except to break; it just gets in the way. I prefer food I can eat directly, without mediation. I am no food server and never will be, though once in a while I pull out one of the old recipes to see what will happen. The oven racks won't sit level, and Cake That Never Fails always occupies its pan on an incline.

The yard was overgrown, unhealthy, and forbidding. Ancient boxy yews shrouded the front windows, obscuring the view in and out. Rimming the lawn were prickly shrubs with little needles that fell off into the grass, where we stepped on them. In the small backyard, bordered by an alley, lilacs struggled up unpruned in perfect shade, with flimsy blossoms on branches like cobwebs. If you touched a petal, it evaporated. In the far corner a detached garage had once stood; someone long ago pulled it down and planted grass. I don't know why he pulled it down, and when I planned my flower garden exactly there I didn't know he had filled in the excavated foundation with stones.

I cleared out the box shrubs in the front. This was real labor, the roots demanding days of digging, shoveling, levering, and prying loose, like hauling old horsehair sofas up from the basement where they've been molding for half a lifetime. Wearing pigskin gloves, I dug out the prickly shrubs and chopped their carcasses into twigs to bag and cart to the curb. I was unearthing our house from its veils of misery, uprooting the bad in life, digging out what didn't grow or what offended or what went bad, making something out of nothing or making nothing out of something, planting what I hoped would fare better. I removed the dead debris I had inherited, trying to make something new, make something my own. Perhaps it was a displacement. It's often enough we can't uproot the rot in our lives, the family relations that don't get better and never will, hurt inflicted and self-inflicted, mistakes made that can't be unmade, injustices with roots too deep and invasive for our small spade to dig out.

Then I planted flowers. What the house needed was color, so much color splashing that no one could identify what grew where. I packed bulbs and seeds into every inch that opened up before the windows and around the lawn. The integrity of each plant was to be breached, the flowers to spill into the grass and spread. The house needed a new story—something bold to fight for its life. It wouldn't happen overnight; it would take time. But why hurry? When I plant, I use a small spade.

Kindly Mrs. Smith next door asks, "Why don't you use a bigger shovel? It would be faster."

"But I want it to take a long time," I tell her. I want to be on my knees, digging small scoops of dirt, looking up at the sky and the trees newly green or flowering. Coming outside, taking off my watch, I want to lose myself in dirt and water. I want to hold my water bucket under the spigot, watch it fill up, and carry it across the yard to the flowers I've just planted.

She looks at me, then walks away shaking her head, her crazy neighbor.

I am not an expert. I belong to no gardener's society, have won no prizes nor witnessed a single flower show. I haven't taken classes or subscribed to magazines. I don't own a gardening book, though I have studied flower catalogs in a state of rapt desire. I have no ambition to have my home listed on the garden tour; I don't want a guide to accompany my plants. I am past instruction. I don't want to know how someone raised perfect irises; whatever that gardener did won't necessarily work for me. I'm quite happy to blunder, to make mistakes. I have to find my own way, and finding that way is at the heart of gardening, the labor of it, the solitude of it, the instincts and messiness of getting a vision down in the ground. When a poppy breaks its furry outer shell and unfurls, it doesn't come with instructions on how to look at it, how to absorb it. I dig holes, I put seeds, bulbs, roots in those holes; I cover them up and wait to see if anything will ferment in the dark, if anything will take hold.

I was unsure what to do with the side yard until Gwen mailed the old dolls back to me in a large box, with a note saying, "It's your daughter's turn." When I lifted the lid, there they were, just as I remembered them, lying stiffly in tissue paper. Not one tiny shoe or hair ribbon missing. The same closed red lips, the same tiny spoons. No chips or nicks, no broken limbs or bald spots. They had not been pulled this way and that in the heat of play until their shape had become something else. The hole in one pair of stockings and a few dirty smudges on their lilac eyelids were the only signs that they had been touched.

I took the box outside and dug a deep hole in the side yard, like a small grave. I laid the dolls directly on the bottom soil, without the box, and then with my bare hands scooped dirt over them. I packed the dirt into their ears and hair, rubbed it all over their pinafores, covering them completely. The dolls had come to the end of the line. To mark the site I planted yarrow—whose yield was immediately staggering until I had to address the question of the weed.

There is a weed on the side of the house in the flower bed where I buried the dolls, and it grows about a foot a day, weaving itself round and round the plants, starting at the base and then climbing in tight knots to the top. It strangles its host.

The flowers I planted were doing very well until I noticed the vine that had suddenly insinuated itself intimately into the garden and was accomplishing its stranglehold. Instinctually I began yanking at the vine, often decapitating the flowers I was trying to save. Everything had been growing so well, I thought, why did this have to happen? Calming down with effort, I realized I had to get at the base of the vine and pull from there, which wasn't easy because of the bushy growth of the yarrow. If I didn't get the vine at the base, I just removed one small link of its coil, restored in moments. When I finally got a view to the soil, I saw the vine was everywhere, growing in robust clusters of tendrils and then radiating out into every plant. Most of the plants were wrapped tightly. Even if I pulled every vine at its base and every runner, I would have only temporarily removed the weed because in the night, when I wasn't looking, it would begin again.

The side yard was being choked to death and there wasn't much to be done about it. At first I was desperate and destroyed as much of my flowers as the weed itself. Then I tried moderation, limiting myself to periods of calm weeding, careful to go after the base. I schooled myself not to think about the weed except at the designated times I had set aside. This worked best for maintaining some peace of mind, but did little for my flowers. It was especially hard because the side yard is right outside the windows where I write. I found myself thinking about what I'd see if I peered out. The truth is that in gardening there is much to contend with, the weed is but one example. It's like a bad plot line that won't happily resolve itself once and for all or the past you think you've left behind that keeps reappearing. Sometimes when two chrysanthemums have bloomed in late summer, side by side, the next year one will come back and the other won't. Why? The same location and the same conditions, one makes it and the other does not. There is death in gardening, mysterious and final. Weedkillers harm as much as help.

Now as an experiment I'm doing nothing or nearly nothing. Spring comes and with it growth, often bigger and better than the year before. Everything seems possible in May and June. Then comes July and the vine. It will either strangle everything in sight or reach some plateau, surfeit of kill, and whatever the outcome I will learn to live with it.

In the backyard it's been a different sort of story. There I had a vision of what I wanted to see, and roses were part of it, and what I call a moon garden. I needed to grow roses to make a life for myself—one concrete thing I could do to that end, like those pioneer women who in settling the wilderness planted flowers despite the odds against them. I can imagine their satisfaction looking at even one surviving morning glory or hollyhock. I wonder what they planted, what pleased them most? Perhaps it was the black hollyhock, deep velvety maroon, sultry, nocturnal, and subversive.

I began in the far corner, digging up what I thought was mere grass and dirt, but came upon stone deposits going down I didn't know how many feet deep. I dug up the layer of soil, then lifted stones into a wheelbarrow and dumped them in our stone driveway alongside the house. Every day for many days I pried out the stones, throwing them into the wheelbarrow. When I was done, I had excavated a hole in need of filling. I stood on its rim, looking down and in. I filled in the hole with peat and soil, getting a good mix. Then I planted the plot of roses, my first. I didn't know what I was doing from start to finish, didn't know what I was excavating, what I was up against, didn't know anything about roses. The spot was imperfect. The bushes tilted up at a slant to escape the shade of an inconvenient tree that grows across the alley. But they produced roses, and that was the thing. I felt I'd be all right if I could bring roses out of stone. I worked hard, ineptly following impulses rather than instruction, but roses grew. I was able to fill the house with roses, give them away. Neighbors liked to walk down the alley to follow my progress from its unpromising beginning.

The moon garden is a long, curving plot, built on the crest of a small incline, not steep but far from level, standing open, free from shade or any interference with the light. I planted the fragrant white lilies of the valley there among the first flowers of spring. All the shades of delphinium, from the deepest purple through royal blues to the pale pacific blues, from lavender to white, intermix in a rainbow of shades, not solid bands of color. White lilies, white peonies, and white phlox massively interlace with the delphiniums. After work, while others cook in hot kitchens, my daughter and I sometimes walk out to the garden, she with her jar of peanuts, I with my gin and tonic, and stretch out on lounge chairs and watch the sun slowly go down over the big tree across the alley. The lights come on all over, and people are just beginning to clean up after dinner, but we can't hear faucets running or dishes being scraped. Not fading into ordinariness as the sun recedes, the flowers become more themselves. In moonlight flowers are soft and dazzling, a virtuosity of color and presence; breathing. My daughter and I see the play of light as the moon appears. In the dark I cannot see her, but I can hear the rustle of her peanuts.

We are there tonight. It is the last day of June; it was a

scorcher, with a dry wind that reminded me of a prairie breeze. No one was mowing lawns or edging; no one was walking a dog or roller-blading, no street hockey today. Even the dogs were quiet, too hot to bother who passed. The sounds were the hum of air conditioners and the dry stir of leaves, a sound as close to rustle as I've heard. The stir of leaves was not continuous like the hum, more a cadence that comes and goes, a gesture of movement.

This morning, before the heat reached its peak, when the petals and leaves had little beads of dew, I cut flowers from around the yard and put them in a blue glass vase on the white kitchen table. I made sure to choose fresh stems, not ones withering on the other side of the crest. I cut four stalks of delphinium, sky blue petals with a white bee. Through the clear blue glass I could see their stems touching bottom and a few tendrils of unopened blooms floating. I cut tickweed, compact, tightly ruffled, their color a strong gold, emphatic and warm. I like tickweed—you cut the dead blooms and it comes back and back. It isn't elegant as delphinium, but when you put the two together, the coarse and the graceful, you begin to get a kind of dissonant beauty.

I was after something unpredictable, made from what's available, not a bouquet you purchase at the florist. I didn't want to replicate it a week from now or next year; I wanted to forget the combination when these flowers died. It's a bouquet of the common and the uncommon, the coarse and the delicate, full blues, bold golds, faint corals. At five o'clock the sunlight was white and brilliant; it made houses look chalky in the distance. The sun was pouring through the three windows of our kitchen on the white tiles of our table, and pooling at the bottom of a bowl empty except for a single lime. Next to it the flowers have been unfolding in the vase all day. They are no longer crisp and have begun to drop their petals, not too much but a little—little pieces of gold like paint dripped on a floor, a rain of blues, a few white centers scattered on the white tiles, like a haiku.

Posture

She's spotted me from the second-story window. She bustles down the stairs and out the door—the screen door slams shut—into the backyard, where I am digging up irises. I watch her walk purposefully toward me, she carries herself high into the world, that bounce in her step I hope she'll never lose, even when she's pitched against some treacherous terrain.

She comes to me across the deck and down into the yard. She has the upright posture my mother wished I had, a swan's neck, a straight back, yet hers is not a remedy. There are no more remedies. The way she holds herself says, *I'm here by right and I'm comfortable.* She hasn't yet encountered anything to chip away at her chances.

She sits down next to me in a pile of leaves. "What are you digging?" she asks. Her voice moves forward in her mouth, rich and velvety.

"These irises didn't bloom last spring. But I think they might next spring if we move them to another spot."

"Why didn't they bloom?"

"I don't know for certain." I show her a large clump of irises that have grown together. "See how the separate bulbs have become one big iris?" She nods. "Well, that isn't healthy. I have to cut them apart, separating them, and then replant them. Where do you think we should move them?"

"In the back corner, by the alley." She pauses. "Are irises those tall flowers that look like birds?"

I laugh at her description. She laughs too. "Your father brought irises to the hospital when you were born, deep purple with gold markings. Now, when I think of irises, I think, *flowers of my daughter's birth*." I did not say, "Before your birth I thought *the veins of my sister's eyelids*."

She sits up straight when she speaks. Her voice is no whisper. "Why did you name me Lily? You could have named me Iris."

I consider how to answer. Given my history with names, there is no simple answer. "We had a hard time deciding what to name you. I preferred names beginning with a consonant. We made a list."

"What names did you think about?"

"I thought about naming you after Helen."

"But she died." Matter-of-fact. I'm glad, and yet hurt a little.

"I always liked the name," I say, walking back toward the corner.

"Why didn't you name me Helen, then?" she asks, following me.

"It seemed already taken."

"Why did you pick Lily?"

"It begins with a letter I love, and has a lilting sound. My mother's favorite flower was lily of the valley. I've always imagined that in the house my sisters and mother lived in before I was born there were beds of lily of the valley." I dig out a place for the iris. "They multiply over the years, and they thrive in sun and shade. A flower for remembering *and* beginning, we thought."

"But we hardly see your mother."

"I remember, nevertheless." The bulb goes in. "I see her in you. You're going to be tall, just as she is, long and slender. You have her wide-set eyes and beautiful bone structure, a forehead like a proud prow."

She looks confused for a moment. "But you are my mother, aren't you? You did give birth to me?"

I laugh again and answer in the affirmative.

She goes back into the house and leaves me to my planting. I think about Fran and Gwen, how as girls they improved themselves along the lines our mother established. They did not deviate. They complied and achieved the proper stance. They could walk balancing a stack of books on their heads. Their bodies were large boxes into which rebellion was stuffed and the lids hooked down. They launched their arrowy necks into the space of adolescence and built roads, straight and narrow, right through to adulthood. Of one sister or the other it was said, "Look at how beautifully she stands." When I had looked to my sisters for guidance, they had seemed pinched, forever contracting themselves into uprightness. The patient positioning held up to me by my sisters did not seem the kind of consequence I sought.

"Marriage," my mother told them, "will furnish you with the proper pedestal upon which to display your training." Their bridal trains draped from erect shoulders to the ground, pooling gracefully, obscuring their feet. They married tall husbands who did not have to bend down to kiss them. My sisters had accepted the correlation between a woman's posture and a woman's stature. It seemed to me that my sisters, having achieved perfect posture, disappeared.

I hope Lily will see the difference.

Hair

I've been around and seen the Taj Mahal and the Grand Canyon and Marilyn Monroe's footprints outside Grauman's Chinese, but I've never seen my mother wash her own hair. After my mother married, she never washed her own hair again. As a girl and an unmarried woman—yes—but, in my lifetime, she never washed her hair with her own two hands. Upon matrimony, she began weekly treks to the beauty salon where Julie washed and styled her hair. Her appointment on Fridays at two o'clock was never canceled or rescheduled; it was the bedrock of her week, around which she pivoted and planned. These two hours were indispensable to my mother's routine, to her sense of herself and what, as a woman, she should concern herself with—not to mention their being her primary source of information about all sorts of things she wouldn't otherwise come to know. With Julie my mother discussed momentous decisions concerning hair color and the advancement of age and what could be done about it, hair length and its effect upon maturity, when to perm and when not to perm, the need to proceed with caution when a woman desperately wanted a major change in her life like dumping her husband or sending back her newborn baby and the only change she could effect was a change in her hair. That was what Julie called a "dangerous time" in a woman's life. When my mother spoke to Julie, she spoke in conspiratorial, almost confessional, tones I had never heard before. Her voice was usually tense, on guard, the laughter forced, but with Julie it dropped much lower, the timbre darker than the upper-register shrills sounded at home. And most remarkably, she listened to everything Julie said.

I was puzzled by the way my mother's sense of self-worth and mood seemed dependent upon how she thought her hair looked, how the search for the perfect hairstyle never ended. Just as my mother seemed to like her latest color and cut, she began to agitate for a new look. The cut seemed to have become a melancholy testimony to time's inexorable passage. Her hair never stood in and of itself; it was always moored to a complex set of needs and desires her hair couldn't in itself satisfy. She wanted her hair to illuminate the relationship between herself and the idea of motion while appearing still, for example. My mother wanted her hair to be fashioned into an event with a complicated narrative past. However, the more my mother attempted to impose a hairstyle pulled from an idealized image of herself, the more the hairstyle seemed to be at odds with my mother. The more the hairstyle became substantial, the more the woman underneath was obscured. She'd riffle through women's magazines and stare for long dreamy hours at a particular woman's coiffure. Then she'd ask my father in an artificially casual voice: "How do you think I'd look with really short hair?" or "Would blond become me?" My father never committed himself to an opinion. He had learned from long experience that no response he made could turn out well; anything he said would be used against him, if not in the immediate circumstances, then down the line, for my mother never forgot anything anyone ever said about her hair. My father's refusal to engage the hair question irritated her.

So, too, I was puzzled to see that unmarried women washed their own hair, and married women, in my mother's circle at least, by some unwritten dictum never touched their own hair. I began studying before-and-after photographs of my mother's friends. These were all the same. In the premarried mode, their hair was soft and unformed. After the wedding, the hairstyles bore the stamp of property, looked constructed from grooming talents not their own, hairstyles I'd call produced, requiring constant upkeep and technique to sustain the considerable loft and rigidity—in short, the antithesis of anything I might naively call natural. This was hair no one touched, crushed, or ran fingers through. One poked and prodded various hair masses back into formation. This hair presented obstacles to embrace; the scent of the hair spray alone warded off man, child, and pests. I never saw my father stroke my mother's head. Children whimpered when my mother came home fresh from the salon with a potent do. Just when a woman's life was supposed to be opening out into daily affection, the sanctioned affection of husband and children, the women of my mother's circle encased themselves in a helmet of hair not unlike Medusa's.

In so-called middle age, my mother's hair never moved, never blew, never fell in her face: her hair became a museum piece. When she went to bed, she wore a blue net, and when she took short showers—short because, after all, she wasn't washing her hair and she was seldom dirty—she wore a blue plastic cap for the sake of preservation. From one appointment to the next, the only change her hair could be said to undergo was to become crestfallen. Taking extended vacations presented problems sufficiently troublesome to rule out countries where she feared no beauty parlors existed. In the beginning, my parents took overnighters, then weeklong jaunts, and thereby avoided the whole hair dilemma. Extending their vacations to two weeks was eventually managed by my mother applying more hair spray and sleeping sitting up. But after the two-week mark had been reached, she was forced to either return home or venture into an unfamiliar salon and subject herself to scrutiny, the kind of scrutiny that leaves no woman unscathed. Then she faced Julie's disapproval, for no matter how expensive and expert the salon, my mother's hair was to be lamented. Speaking just for myself, I had difficulty distinguishing Julie's cunning from the stranger's. In these years my mother's hair looked curled, teased, and sprayed into a wave-tossed monument with holes poked through for glasses. She believed the damage done to her hair was tangible proof she had been somewhere, like stickers on her suitcases.

My sisters have worked out their hair positions differently. Fran's solution has been to fix upon one hairstyle and never change it. She wants to be thought of in a singular fashion. As time goes on, this style becomes more and more a sort of *no*. She may vary the length from long to longer, but that is the extent of her alteration. Once after having her first baby, the dangerous time for women, she recklessly cut her hair to just below the ear. She immediately regretted the decision and began growing it back as she walked home from the salon, vowing not to repeat the mistake. Her signature is dark, straight hair pulled heavily off her face in a large silver clip, found at any Woolworth's. When one clip breaks, she buys another just like it. My mother hates the timelessness of my sister's hair. She equates it with a refusal to face growing old.

My mother says, "It's immature to wear your hair the same way all your life."

Fran replies, "It's immature to never stop thinking about your hair. If this hairstyle was good enough when I was twenty, it's good enough when I'm forty, if not better."

"But what about change?" my mother asks.

"Change is overrated," Fran says, flipping her long hair over her shoulder definitively. "I feel my hair."

Gwen was born with thin, lifeless, nondescript hair: a cross she has had to bear. Even in the few baby pictures, the limp strands plastered on her forehead in question marks wear her down. Shame and self-effacement are especially plain in the pictures where she posed with Fran, whose dark hair dominates the frame. Gwen's spent her life attempting to disguise the real state of her hair. Some years she'd focus on style, pulling it back in ponytails so that from the front no one could see there wasn't much hair in the back. She tried artless, even messy styles— as if she had just tied it up any old way before taking a bath or bunched it to look deliberately snarled. There were the weird years punctuated by styles that looked as if she had taken sugar water and lemon juice and squeezed them onto her wet hair and then let them crystallize. The worst style was when she took her hair and piled it on the top of her head in a cone shape and then crimped the ponytail into a zigzag. Personally, I thought she had gone too far. No single approach solved the hair problem, and so now, in maturity, she combines the various phases of attack in hope something will work. She frosts both the gray strands and the pale brown and then perms for added body and thickness. She's forced to keep her hair short because chemicals do tend to destroy. My mother admires Gwen's determination to transform herself, and never more than in her latest assault upon age. No one has seen for many years, nor does anyone remember, what the untreated color or texture of either my mother's or my sister's hair might be.

Because I was the youngest by many years, there was little to distract my mother's considerable attention from the problem of my hair. I had cowlicks, a remarkable number of them, which like little arrows shot across my scalp. They refused to be trained, to lie down quietly in the same direction as the rest of my hair. One at the front insisted on sticking straight up, while two on either side of my ears jutted out seeking sun. The lack of uniformity, the fact that my hair had a mind of its own, infuriated my mother, and she saw to it that Julie cut my hair as short as possible in order to curtail its wanton expression. Sitting in the swivel chair before the mirror while Julie snipped, I felt invisible, as if I were unattached to my hair.

Just when I started to menstruate, my mother decided the battle plan needed a change, and presto, the pageboy replaced the pixie. Since I had not outgrown the thicket of cowlicks, my mother bought a spectrum of brightly colored stretch bands to hold my hair off my face. Then she attached thin pink plastic curlers with snap-on lids to the ends of my hair to make them flip up or under, depending on her mood. The stretch bands pressed my hair flat until the very bottom, at which point the ends formed a tunnel with ridges from the roller caps—a point of emphasis, she called it. Coupled with the aquamarine eye-glasses, newly acquired, I looked like an overgrown insect that had none of its kind to bond with.

However, I was not alone. Unless you were the last in a long line of sisters, chances were good that your hair would not go unnoticed by your mother. Each of my friends was subjected to her mother's hair dictatorship, although with entirely different results. Perry Jensen's mother insisted that all five of her daughters peroxide their hair blond and pull it into high ponytails. All the girls' hair turned green in the summer from chlorine. Melissa Matson underwent a look-alike home perm with her mother, an experience she never did recover from. She developed a phobic reaction to anything synthetic, which made life very expensive. Not only did mother and daughter have identical tight curls and wear mother-daughter outfits, later they had look-alike nose jobs.

In my generation, many women who survived hair bondage to their mothers now experiment with hairstyles as one would test a new design: to see how it works, what it will withstand, and how it can be improved. Testing requires boldness, for often the style fails dramatically, as when I had my hair cut about a half inch long at the top, and it stood straight up like a tacky shag carpet. I had to live with the results, bear daily witness to the kinks in its design for nine months until strategies of damage control could be deployed. But sometimes women I know create a look that startles in its originality and suggests a future not yet realized.

The women in my family divide into two general groups: those who fasten upon one style, become identified with a look, and are impervious to change, weathering the years steadfastly, and those who, for a variety of reasons, are in the business of transforming themselves. In Gwen's case, the quest for perfect hair originates in a need to mask her own appearance; in my mother's case, she wants to achieve a beauty of person unavailable in her own life story. Some women seek transformation, not because they are dissatisfied with themselves, but because hair change is a means of moving along in their lives. These women create portraits of themselves that won't last forever; a new hairstyle will write over the last.

Since my mother dictated my hair, I never took a stand on the hair issue. In maturity, I'm incapable of assuming a coherent or consistent philosophy. I have wayward hair: it's always becoming something else. The moment it arrives at a recognizable style, it begins to undo itself, it grows, the sun colors it, it waves. When one hairpin goes in, another seems to come out. Sometimes I think I should follow Fran—she claims to never give more than a passing thought to her hair and can't see what all the angst is about.

She asks, "Don't women have better things to think about than their hair?"

I bite back, "But don't you think hair should show who you are?"

"To be honest, I've never thought about it. I don't think so. Cut your hair the same way, and lose yourself in something else. You're distracted from the real action."

I want to do what my sister says, but when I walk out into shop-lined streets, I automatically study women's hair and always with the same question: How did they arrive at their hair?

Lately I've been feeling more and more like my mother. I hadn't known how to resolve the dilemma until I found Rhonda. I don't know if I found Rhonda or made her up. She is not a normally trained hairdresser: she has a different set of eyes, unaffected. One day while out driving around to no place in particular, at the bottom of a hill I found "Rhonda's Hair Salon—Don't Look Back" written on a life-size cardboard image of Rhonda. Her shop was on the top of this steep, orchard-planted hill, on a plateau with a great view that opened out and went on forever. I parked my motorcycle at the bottom and walked up. Zigzagging all the way up the hill, leaning against or sticking out from behind the apple trees, were more life-sized cardboard likenesses of Rhonda. Except for the explosive sunbursts in her hair, no two signs were the same. At the bottom, she wore long red hair falling below her knees and covering her entire body like a shawl. As I climbed the hill, Rhonda's hair gradually became shorter and shorter, and each length was cut differently, until, when I reached the top, her head was shaved and glistening in the sun. I found Rhonda herself out under one of the apple trees wearing running shoes. Her hair was long and red and looked as if it had never been cut.

I had made no appointment. She didn't seem to have any business at the moment. Was she waiting for me? She motioned me inside her shop and told me she had no aspirations to be a hairdresser; she just fell into it. "I see hair," she continued, "as an extension of the head, and therefore I try to do hair with a lot of thought." Inside not a single strand of hair floated upon the floor. She had a voice you could get lost in. It was a voice that said, Come to me, but don't stay. Never stay. It said, You have to keep moving: I am just a stop along the way.

She said, "Nothing is permanent, nothing is forever. Don't feel hampered or hemmed in by the shape of your face or the shape of your past. Hair is vital, sustains mistakes, can be born again. You don't have to marry it. Now tip back and put your head into my hands."

Hands

And what of loss? Others might speak of it; we would not. We were to suffer it silently.

The unspeakable.

At Helen's funeral, I overheard my mother's friends, whispering. They huddled in the corner of the living room. Alone in the immense room, empty but for the vase of flowers swimming in what seemed a mist.

Those women squeezed themselves into the corner, for the room had begun to shrink.

They spoke of the loss my mother had suffered. *The loss she suffered*— the phrase buried, planted in my brain, available still at a moment's notice.

I did not choose to be lessened.

It was then I began to see my mother as withered, wasting away, the flesh falling away simply. It was then I began to make lists of what her losses might have been and to see her world constrict around her. What tears at me is this—that the water spills against our will. It's as if I've been carrying water to my mouth in my hands. The water pools in my hands, which I lift to my bending,

The crude bones of my wrist lay limpidly by my side.

There is no glass. It doesn't exist.

waiting mouth. I've never been not thirsty. Midway my hands begin to shake. They sweat with the effort to steady them. Though I concentrate on lifting them, commanding them to rise, they will not. The water splashes over the human rim of flesh, dripping slowly in large, obscene drops onto the floor.

The water quakes in the cup of my hands.

Everything spills.

My mother would not hold onto Helen's possessions. In the spring, when the forsythia bloomed, she lopped off the branches with her shears. Carrying heavy armfuls, she roamed the streets, giving them away. She would return tired.

Keeping one step ahead of loss.

The desire came over me to cover my mother, throw shawls about her shoulders as she passed into the kitchen, make sure she had a blanket at night.

I made my own list of losses, images that I have worked hard to forget—what Helen looked like, the cat caught in the trap. The machine of repetition, taking away, of having and not having. These images have blurred into a thirst.

The cat's name was May. I remember.

To cup both hands together

and fill with clean, cold water, to lift those hands to my lips and drink

without spilling a drop;

to turn to you

and for you to turn to me

and for us to be face to face

                                mother and daughter

sister and sister

                                daughter and mother

                     sister,   *sister.*

Woman Walking

I like to walk to the post office, carrying my letter in my hand, taking a long while to get there. I like to give my letter to a clerk, to see it weighed and make sure the postage is right. It is good to walk all the way, being careful not to drop the envelope or smudge the address, recalling what I have written, noticing that the stamp is crooked, but pleased that it is well chosen. I do not drive—so few minutes to whisk away what I have labored over through many interruptions. It should take time to mail a letter. I spend my breath and then stand in line, feeling my pulse calm down, waiting my turn. I walk to be unhoused, to reacquaint myself with the movements of my heart.

One Saturday morning, a windy and beautiful day, I carried what had been a difficult letter to write, written to a friend made more alone by sudden illness than anyone should be. A man paused in his mowing to watch me. I had seen him before, many times. From a distance he looked portly and old, with movements slow and careful. He wore an old-fashioned hat, a straw Dutch sun hat that made his head look bland. Closer he looked younger, his head childlike.

Coming adjacent on his riding mower, he took off his hat and said, "Is it blue enough for you?"

What kind of question was this? Should I say no, I want the day blue as a blue racer darting quick through ferns, or the blue of varicose veins knotted down an old woman's legs? Or the pale blue of wisteria festooned across the night? Midnight milk we'll never drink. What could I answer?

He wanted me to stay. He had started looking for me, calculating when I walked, getting a story or joke ready.

I didn't smile, thinking, I'm walking, leave me alone. I'm walking to get away; I don't want you to be wanting anything from me.

He didn't get it. He tried to talk to me anyway. As I walked away, my steps felt heavy with the connection I had refused. I wondered if I'd have to walk another route.

At the post office a man and a woman ahead of me dumped a big parcel on the counter and tried to pay the postage with a check.

The clerk, a young woman, asked to see a driver's license.

The woman had no license on her person.

But she had driven, the clerk pointed out.

She had left it in the car, she said, and she was *not* going to go get it.

In apologetic tones the clerk recited the post office's policy.

The couple started yelling. The yelling made them look very sunburned. They swore obscenities in unison. The line grew longer, and customers behind me began to blow up. The clerk stated the regulations; the couple spewed out hatred at the clerk; the people in line shouted at the couple. A whole chain letter of anger was getting started. It seemed unsocial not to join in.

At last the couple left, the man tossing a last vulgarity over his shoulder.

The clerk said, "Next."

I dropped out of line, walked out to the foyer, and stabbed my letter into the mail slot.

They cover the town, the merchants' strip with its shops unprosperous or hopeful, the neighborhoods of foursquare houses and rambling schools, the campus rabid with cars, the rumbling truck routes and pitted bridge eternally closed for repairs. They look at the town from on high; they see it from the depths of the

*riverbed. No walk is on the level, for the hills never end; every-
thing goes up and down, and sometimes the incline is sharp and
strenuous. On the steepest path they never run out of breath.
They have a route and a pace, and everyone knows them, knows
their speed and their cut through town.*

Down the street, a man driving an old blue Impala stopped
me. He was probably in his early thirties. "You walk this way a
lot, don't you?" he asked. "I've seen you."

I hesitated. How did he know, and what business was it of
his? Was he following me? I looked around. There was no one
out on the sidewalks, though it was near noon. A car passed. I
moved reluctantly toward the curb and said, "Yes."

"I live right over here on Prospect Path," he said, pointing to
a spot where the street took a bend. "I've lost my cat. It's a white
cat, all white. Have you seen it?"

"Have I seen it?" I asked back in a daze. "No, I haven't. I
haven't seen any white cats this morning."

"I got it from my ex-wife two days ago. She couldn't keep it, and
now I've already lost it. Two days. My kids are going to fall to
pieces when they hear. My wife didn't want to give it to me because
she said I couldn't take care of anything. I guess she's right. I just
live over there. I thought with you walking this way so much
maybe you'd be able to help me, maybe you'd have seen it."

I shook my head no, back and forth.

"What do you think I should do? Do you think the cat's trying to get home to my ex-wife?"

I couldn't help him. Even if I found the cat, it wouldn't solve
the problem. He was going to lose it again, and the ex-wife was-
n't going to improve her opinion of him. She wasn't going to
let him come home. He would have to make his own home, and
it wasn't going to be easy. "Yes," I said, "some cats don't adjust
to being moved. They try to get back where they began. Have
you put up signs? Have you searched the park?"

"Yes," he said, with the cars driving past us. "No. Will you
look for it? I live at 418 Prospect Path."

"Yes," I said. "Yes I will. What's the cat's name?"

"Snowball, my kids named her."

The next day I looked for his signs; there were none.

I walk streets where every step is seen. All my routes are populated; variations are limited; people have come to recognize me. It is not always a happy recognition. I am stopped, intruded upon; I witness episodes I don't want to see and can do nothing about. They are impossible to avoid, and yet they startle me with their sudden appearance. They seem to explode with each touch of my foot on the sidewalk, and even if I hurry by, embarrassed by something private, I carry the sight with me, bring it home. I am so susceptible. There are scenes in my own life I am walking to forget. I had thought walking was anonymous and solitary, that I would set out and see no one, covering random miles of uncultivated land. I thought my resources resided in my feet, that I might circle the block a million times. Even when I faltered, my feet would smell like roots and sprout tendrils.

They like to wave to the people, to know the condition of the sidewalks and time the traffic lights. Their walking is a caress of their town of birth, a claim on their place in the world. They have no interest in what surprise might lie outside their circle. Men snicker and call out and honk their horns to startle them just before they come alongside. It isn't that they don't notice, and they never become accustomed. But they will not vary their route; the same is so important, each day, each week, each year. They follow the familiar and note the changes within. There are job upheavals, illnesses, heartbreaks, marriages, children. But above all else there is walking.

From Prospect Path my route leads me past a house where one night I saw a father, I took him to be the father, who was herding his children into the van in the driveway. There were two, a boy and a girl. Something was wrong. The man was flushed with impatience. He stretched his arms like a bird of prey, trying to clutch them. But they eluded him—the girl ran behind the van, where I couldn't see her, and the boy threw himself down on a large stone in the front corner of the yard. He buried his head in his arms and called to his sister.

From across the street I felt afraid.

The father chased around to the other side of the van, and the girl came back, running to her brother, and they covered the stone with their bodies. The man stalked them, his shoulders rigid, arms unmoving. But before he got to the stone, the children stood up, and the boy put his arm around the girl's shoulders. The man shoved them along with his fists in the smalls of their backs, and they got into the van, crying.

They have each other, I thought. I went on, and my legs pulled at each other stiffly, two faltering things. I stopped at intervals, out of breath. I was walking on the rim of tears.

I used to observe the woman across the alley coming out her back door every afternoon at four-thirty, setting off at a fast pace, and then returning seventy-five minutes later, much more slowly. When she set off, her expression was slightly grim; she returned beatific. One day I asked her where she went. When she said that she walked with her sister, I realized who she was, one of the famous walking sisters, unrecognizable alone. She said that if I could fall in with them, if I made their method mine, I could walk with them. I had to come up to speed fast, because they allowed no one to slow them down. The first time I joined them, in July, I passed out by the water fountain in the post office.

Then through one last neighborhood, where once I spotted smoke drifting out of the second-floor window of the house next to the corner. I ran over to warn whoever was inside, but no one answered the doorbell, and the doors were locked. Neighbors said there was a pet cat, and we tried all the windows and garage, but they too were locked. We were relieved to see the fire engines roar up, and then the fire was out. We stood around and watched them in their thick boots and coats rolling up the heavy hoses.

The next day I read in the newspaper that they had found a woman's body upstairs, on the bathroom floor. She had doused her bed with something, lay on it, and struck a match. The authorities speculated that she had tried to get to the tub to put the flames out. She was fifty-eight, children grown, living with a cat. The neighbors remarked that her yard was always neatly kept.

In the days that followed experts in the clean-up of smoke damage arrived with a driveway-size dumpster. There was even a garage sale.

From her neighborhood I climb up the hills on the back streets. I follow less-known roads away from the fumes and the noise, where once I stumbled onto a dirt path set back behind the public route, shrouded in a hillside of uncleared trees and shrubs. I follow this road to a house that, when I first saw it, stopped me in my tracks and beckoned me to stay. It reminded me of the house on Twenty-second street. I go back to this house set in the unplanned darkness of wild raspberry thickets, the havoc of weeds. Its white paint is peeling; once-black shutters hang by a nail; screens are eaten through. In the overgrown side yard sits a picnic table and benches, as if any moment a family will bound out of the house, a mother carrying glasses of lemonade. Voices. "Girls! Girls! Girls!" the mother calls. Grass has grown unchecked, and any movement to the table would be slow and difficult. I imagine girls emerging from that house. Hula hoops. They would have to hack a path to the table; they would need to have a real desire to get there. I want to stretch my arms across the table to them, sitting on the other side. Our lives barely touched before my sisters were gone. Our hoops almost touched, our worlds almost touched, our lives. For a few moments only, my girlhood met theirs, and then suddenly they were gone. I drink the lemonade from decades ago, still cool in the green darkness. Some afternoons I fall asleep, dreaming of the endless weight of water.

Walking home I have no idea how long I have been gone. It is a shock to discover I am no longer that girl whose hula hoop spun in orbit in the side yard with her sisters defiantly disregarding our mother's calls. "Chores, piano, bedrooms!" Our hula hoops had fallen to earth. Dark fills the sky. Through the lit windows of my house, I see my own family preparing dinner in the kitchen, and they seem strangers. How have I traveled such a distance, leaving one home to make another? I circle the block many times before I can go in.

When I join them, we arrive home from work, change our clothes, and shoot out the back door, leaving children, phone messages, dirty houses. Our first leg slopes down the alley and then onto High Street, pitching us down as on a mission of mercy. There is no warm-up; we start at the top and stay there. We walk until we see her sister in the distance, crossing the bridge. We link up, and the three of us, spanning the sidewalk, head up High.

Women have been walking a long time. They have been shifting their weight from left to right, right to left, for a long time. They have been getting calloused feet, strings and wires of pain shooting up from their ankles, carrying loads of one kind or another, water, babies, food, death; they have carried it on their heads, their backs, in their arms, across vacant lots filled with Queen Anne's Lace, by side yards of clotheslines on which sheets twist and sometimes fall into the mud. Walking isn't a mechanical thing, despite what people think. It isn't just step, stop, step, stop. You can't assume your legs are simply there like underlings, waiting for a command. I was taught how to say please and thank you; no one taught me how to walk in this world. You have to be inclined, and sometimes I lose my inclination. During the night the stitching in my legs comes out. It's as if I have lost my knees—no bending, no flexing, my legs like rods running from my crotch to my feet. No forward drive or purpose. All that is despairing in me concludes in my feet. I am alive, but not quite sure I want to be.

This morning, thinking about that woman and the fire, I remembered when such a fate seemed not unimaginable as my own. When Lily came into my room to see why I wasn't up, she said, "Momma, it's time to get up. It's time."

I whispered, "I'm thinking about it."

She wants to save someone from disaster. She plots stories that imperil her stuffed animals. The curtains catch fire, sputtering up, and she rushes in to save the day, carrying each animal to safety in a towel. She opens her doctor's bag, applies cold compresses to the burns, bandages heads, fans them. Secret Rescue, she calls it. She wants to be a firefighter and has asked for the uniform for her birthday. With this she is saying, I want to be useful and brave. Lily believes her hands have the power to revive life.

She said, "You've been thinking long enough. It's time now to get up and start walking."

Stalling, I said, "We'll see."

"No. It's time. I'll help you." She pulled off the bedcovers and put her hands on my knees. I felt her heat. "How about a walk now?"

"Where are we going?"

On the days I walk alone, I do not travel that route; it depends on their company. But I have become known by joining them.

I remember my grandmother. She once walked with a cane, but I never saw her walk. I remember her in a wheelchair. Her legs were swollen and twisted; they would not support her. They had to be turned and placed, lifted with the hands, pushed roughly to the side. You can tell the life from the legs, the feet, and the toes. She once said, "Make sure your legs tell a good story."

Last summer Lily and I traveled to her grave, and on a beautiful quiet evening planted geraniums. Most of the stones in the cemetery lay in pairs, husband and wife, two hands clasped in prayer, between the arrowed hearts. At the family plot I took my gardening tools and tapped caskets to make a count. A couple more could squeeze in, but not side by side, more like bookends with lots of reading material between. My grandfather's headstone, though next to my grandmother's, lies parallel to something else, a black heartland. My grandmother makes do, a little solitary.

Mushrooms like fists poked up through her grave. Lily and I pulled them out, yanked whatever weed it was that raveled round and round the headstone, and stuffed it in a paper bag. I tried not to step unthoughtfully on the graves covered over by grass. We troweled out holes for more geraniums and planted them, tamping the black earth down with our hands. The work done, I thought of the future. I hoped that some August evening like that one, when the sky has receded and the trees are beautiful in a light reflected from everywhere, my daughter will walk boldly over me.

Acknowledgments

A first book does not arrive on the shelf without people who helped make it happen. Many have moved behind the scenes to bring this book forward. Thanks to those writers, scholars, and friends all—Gail Adams, Pat Foltz, Leigh Gilmore, and Anita Skeen.

Thanks to John Witte, editor of the *Northwest Review*, where many of these chapters had their first airing. He has been my ideal editor; the third eye. And thanks to Robert Atwan, editor of *The Best American Essays* series, who has been instrumental in creating an audience for the contemporary essay.

In the final stages no one could be more fortunate than I in their agent and editor. Elyse Cheney and Jill Bialosky are exemplary of what the publishing world can be—a world of committed individuals who are motivated by the permanence that language and form can create and who work hard on publishing's behalf. My thanks to them are many and true.